East Window

W.S. Merwin

EAST WINDOW

The Asian Translations

COPPER CANYON PRESS
Port Townsend, Washington

Printed in the United States of America.

The publication of this book was supported by grants from the
Lannan Foundation, the National Endowment for the Arts, and
the Washington State Arts Commission. Additional support was received
from Elliott Bay Book Company, Cynthia Hartwig, and the many members
who joined the Friends of Copper Canyon Press. Copper Canyon Press is in
residence with Centrum at Fort Worden State Park.

Copper Canyon Press acknowledges the Seattle Art Museum,
Eugene Fuller Memorial Collection for the use of the cover image:
Crow Screen, ink on paper, gold on silk, Edo Period, circa 1650.

LIBRARY OF CONGRESS CATALOGING-IN-PUBLICATION DATA

Merwin, W.S. (William Stanley), 1927–
East window: the Asian translations / W.S. Merwin.
p. cm.
A collection of selected poems translated by the author
from a variety of Asian languages. Includes index.
ISBN 1-55659-091-1
1. Oriental poetry – Translations into English.
1. Title. PJ418.M57 1998
98-40192
CIP

COPPER CANYON PRESS
Post Office Box 271
Port Townsend, Washington 98368

Contents

Asian Figures

Sun at Midnight: Poems by Musō Soseki

East Window

Preface

These poems, taken from *Selected Translations 1948–1968, Asian Figures, Selected Translations 1968–1978,* and *Sun at Midnight,* represent my attempts to make poetry in English out of poems originally written in Asian languages, over a period of more than three decades. I cannot remember when I first encountered Asian poetry, but it was in translation, of course, because I know no Asian languages. When I was still a child I found, in the Harvard Classics, Edward FitzGerald's version of the *Rubáiyát of Omar Khayyám* – the original language not, according to some definitions, strictly Asian, and the rendering, I am told, a distant approximation, but I have remained fond of it ever since, as a great piece of Victorian poetry. By the time I was sixteen or so I had found Arthur Waley's Chinese translations, and then Pound, and was captivated by them both. Their relations to the forms and the life of the originals I will never be able to assess. But from the originals, by means and with aspirations that were, in certain respects, quite new, they made something new in English, they revealed a whole new range of possibility for poetry in English. Poetry in our language has never been the same since, and all of us are indebted to Waley and Pound whether we recognize it and acknowledge it or not. Their work suggested, among other things, that the relation between translation and the original was more complicated and less definite than had often been assumed. But in fact the notion of what translation really was or could be had been undergoing change all through the nineteenth century, partly as a result of efforts to bring over into English a growing range and variety of originals. The assumptions inherent in the word "translation" had shifted radically since the early eighteenth century.

When Pope set out to translate Homer almost everything (as it appears to us) was known beforehand. He knew who most of his immediate readers would be: they had subscribed for the translations. They, in turn, knew – or thought they knew – who Homer was, and they knew the text, in the original. Both the subscribers and the translator took it for granted that the proper form for heroic verse, in English, must of course be the heroic couplet. Pope's work was expected to display the wit, elegance, and brilliance with which he could render a generally accepted notion of the Homeric poems into a familiar English verse form.

Since the eighteenth century, and especially since the beginning of modernism, more and more translations have been undertaken with the clear purpose of introducing readers (most of them, of course, unknown to the translators) to works they could not read in the original, by authors they might very well never have heard of, from cultures, traditions, and forms with which they had no acquaintance. The contrast with Pope's situation is completed by the phenomenon that has appeared with growing frequency in the past half century, of poet-translators who do not, themselves, know the language from which they are making their versions, but must rely, for their grasp of the originals, on the knowledge and work of others.

New – or different – assumptions mean different risks. New assumptions about the meaning of the word "translation," whether or not they are defined, imply different aspects of the basic risk of all translation, however that is conceived. Which is no risk at all, in terms of the most common cliché on the subject: that all translation is impossible. We seem to need it, just the same, insofar as we need literature at all. In our time, an individual or social literary culture without it is unthinkable. What is it that we think we need? We begin with the idea that it is the original – which means our relative conception of the original, as scholars, potential translators, or readers. At the outset, the notion is probably not consciously involved with any thought of the available means of translation. The "original" may even figure as something that might exist in more forms than one, just as it can be understood by more than one reader. But if we take a single word of any language and try to find an exact equivalent in another, even if the second language is closely akin to the first, we have to admit that it cannot be done. A single primary denotation may be shared, but the constellation of secondary meanings, the moving rings of associations, the etymological echoes, the sound and its own levels of association, do not have an equivalent because they cannot. If we put two words of a language together and repeat the attempt, the failure is obvious. Yet if we continue, we reach a point where some sequence of the first language conveys a dynamic unit, a rudiment of form. Some energy of the first language begins to be manifest, not only in single words but in the charge of their relationship. The surprising thing is that at this point the hope of translation does not fade altogether, but begins to emerge. Not that these rudiments of form in the original language can be matched – any more than individual words could be – with exact equivalents in another. But the imaginative force that they embody, and that single words embody in context, may suggest convocations of words in another language that will have a comparable thrust and sense.

By "rudiments of form" I mean recognizable elements of verbal order, not verse forms. I began with what I suppose was, and perhaps still is, an unusual preconception about the latter: the fidelity in translating a poem should include an ambition to reproduce the original verse form. Besides, I started translating partly as a discipline, hoping that the process might help me to learn to write. Pound was one of the first to recommend the practice to me. I went to visit him at St. Elizabeth's in the forties, when I was a student. He urged me to "get as close to the original as possible," and told me to keep the rhyme scheme of the poem I was translating, too, if I could, for the exercise as much as anything else. He was generous. And eloquent about what the practice could teach about the possibilities of English. He recommended that I should look, just then, at the Spanish *romancero*, and I did; but it was almost fifteen years before I actually made versions of many of the *romances* – and without the original rhyme schemes. I kept to his advice, at the time. When I did come, gradually, to abandon more and more often the verse forms of poems that I was translating, I did not try to formulate a precise principle for doing so. Translation is a fairly

empirical practice, usually, and the "reasons" for making par-
ticular choices, however well-grounded in scholarship, are sel-
dom wholly explicable. I would have recognized, probably quite
early, a simple reluctance to sacrifice imagined felicities of the
potential English version, to keep a verse pattern that was, in a
sense, abstract. The preference seems to me practical, at least.
I think I began to consider the subject more systematically
when I was trying to decide on the best form for a translation
of the *Chanson de Roland*. I had before me versions in blank
verse both regular and more or less free, and one that contrived
to keep not only the metrical structure of the Old French but
the rhyme scheme: verse paragraphs known as *laisses*, some-
times many lines in length, each line ending with the same as-
sonance. The result, in English, struck me as nothing more
than an intellectual curiosity; unreadable. The word order of
the lifeless English was contorted, line by line, to get those
sounds to come out right. As for the virtues of the original that
had moved hearers for centuries and contributed to the poem's
survival over a thousand years, there was scarcely an indication
of what they might have been. It's easy to multiply examples of
this kind of translation. And yet it must be true that in trans-
lating, as in writing, formal verse, exigencies of the form itself
occasionally contribute to the tension and resonance of the lan-
guage. But I realized at some point that I had come to consider
the verse conventions of original poems as part of the original
language, in which they had a history of associations like that
of individual words – something impossible to suggest in En-
glish simply by repeating the forms. Verse conventions are to a

large degree matters of effects, which depend on a familiarity that cannot, of course, be translated at all. The effects of the convention in the new language can never be those it produces in the former one. This is true even with forms that have already been adopted. There would be certain obvious advantages in retaining the sonnet form in English, if translating a sonnet from Italian, but however successful the result, the sonnet form in English does not have the same associations it has in Italian; its effect is not the same; it does not mean the same thing. And sometimes an apparent similarity of form can be utterly misleading. The *Chanson de Roland*, again, for example. The original is in a ten-syllable line, and an English-speaking translator would naturally think, at first, of iambic pentameter. But if the poem is translated into any sort of blank verse in English (leaving aside the question of the relative vitality and brightness of that form in our age), the result is bound to evoke reverberations of the pentameter line in English from Marlowe through Tennyson – echoes that drown the real effect and value of the Old French verse.

The whole practice is based on paradox: wanting the original leads us to want a translation. And the very notion of making or using a translation implies that it will not and cannot be the original. It must be something else. The original assumes the status of an impossible ideal, and our actual demands must concern themselves with the differences from it, with the manner of standing instead of it. When I tried to formulate practically what I wanted of a translation, whether by someone else or by me, it was something like this: without deliberately altering the overt meaning of the original poem, I wanted the translation to represent, with as much life as possible, some aspect, some quality of the poem that made the translator think it was worth translating in the first place. I know I arrived at this apparently simple criterion by a process of elimination, remembering all the translations – whatever their other virtues – that I had read, or read at, and set down, thinking, "If the original is really *like* that, what could have been the point of translating it?"

The quality that is conveyed to represent the original is bound to differ with different translators, which is both a hazard and an opportunity. In the ideal sense in which one wants only the original, one wants the translator not to exist at all. In the practical sense in which the demand takes into account the nature of translation, the gifts – such as they are – of the translator are inescapably important. A poet-translator cannot write with any authority using someone else's way of hearing.

I have not set out to make translations that distorted the meaning of the originals on pretext of some other overriding originality. For several years I tried to maintain illogical barriers between what I translated and "my own" writing, and I think the insistence on the distinction was better than indulging in a view of everything being the (presumably inspired) same. But no single thing that anyone does is wholly separate from any other, and impulses, hopes, predilections toward writings as yet unconceived certainly must have manifested themselves in the choices of poems from other languages that I preferred to read and wanted to translate, and in the ways that I went about both. And whatever is done, translation included, obviously has some effect on what is written afterward. Except in a very few cases, it would be hard for me to trace in subsequent writings of my own the influence of particular translations that I have made, but I know that the influences were and are there. The work of translation did teach, in the sense of forming, and making available, ways of hearing.

In the translations in *Asian Figures*, I let the sequence of the ideograms (which in most cases I had in front of me, with their transliterations) suggest the English word order, where that could be done without destroying the sense. The series of translations from Ghalib, made from literal versions, scholarly material, and direct guidance supplied by Aijaz Ahmad, were part of the same impulse. My first drafts remained close to the original ghazal form, and both Aijaz and I thought them papery. As he planned to include in the eventual publication the original texts, literal versions, and his notes on vocabulary, the whole point of the enterprise was to produce something else from the material – poems in English, if possible. The rule was that they were not to conflict with Ghalib's meaning, phrase by phrase, but that they need not render everything, either. Translation was viewed as fragmentary in any case; one could choose the fragments, to some degree. Considering the inadequacy of any approach to translation, I had been thinking of Cézanne's painting the Montagne Sainte Victoire over and over, each painting new, each one another mountain, each one different from the one he had started to paint. I imagined that in translating a poem something might be gained by making a series of versions bringing out different possibilities. I still think so, though I realize that versions, however many, from a single poet-translator are likely to sound like variants of each other, and echo the translator's ear at least as clearly as they do the original.

The Ghalib translations are among those made without any firsthand knowledge of the original language, as I have explained. I don't know that such a procedure can either be justified or condemned altogether, any more than translation as a whole can be. Auden, for one, thought it the best possible way of going about it. I suspect it depends on the circumstances – who is doing the work, and the collaborators' relation to each other and to the poetry they are translating. I have had my doubts about working this way, and have resolved several times not to do any more translation of this kind (as I have resolved not to translate any more at all), but I have succumbed repeatedly to particular material.

I should make it clear that the only languages from which I can translate directly are Romance languages, and that I am less familiar with Italian and Portuguese than with French and Spanish. All the translations in this collection were based on someone else's knowledge. I continued to go about this in different ways, certain that no one translation will be absolute, for the obvious reason that it cannot be the original, and the original, as long as anyone is interested in it, will be heard in ways that gradually come to differ more and more among readers who use the second language in changing ways.

After 1978, my principal attempt at translation from an Asian language was the collaboration with Sōiku Shigematsu on the poems of Musō. I met Shigematsu-sensei in 1976, and we began talking about Musō, as I remember, almost at once. For years I had been interested in what I had read of Japanese poetry from the earliest period through Bashō and his disciples, and in the relation between much of the poetry and Buddhist insight. Shigematsu-sensei is a Rinzai priest and a professor of American literature (particularly the Transcendentalists) in Japan, who had been working on literal versions of Musō's poems for years and was looking for a poet with whom he could collaborate in English. We worked together over Musō's poems, mostly by correspondence, for over a decade.

When I look back at the various attempts to make in English something whose life seemed to me to suggest what was alive in the original, I am not sure that "translation" is the right word for some of the ways of trying that, but no other term seems adequate either, and the restless search for one becomes part of the practice of translation, an enterprise that is plainly impossible and nevertheless indispensable. The fond hope that has led me is fed by the same spring, I think, that sustains poetry and language itself.

–W.S.M.

SELECTED TRANSLATIONS

Oh the sound of her silk sleeves
no longer
oh the dust deepening
in the jade courtyard
the vacant room cold
abandoned
the doors
double-barred and their bars
littered with fallen leaves
oh if anyone looks now
for the beauty
of that woman where can it be found
I feel my heart
to which rest will not come

The Lake of the Ten Thousand Mountains

I throw the line in from this little island.
The water is clear and my heart is protected.
The fish pass under the trees of the lake.
Along the promontory monkeys swing on the vines.
The wandering beauty of former days took off her necklace
in these mountains, the legend says.
I look for her but I have not found her.
The songs of the rowers lose the way to the moon.

Quiet Night Thoughts

I wake and my bed is gleaming with moonlight

Frozen into the dazzling whiteness I look up
To the moon herself
And lie thinking of home

Where the mist has torn
The hills are the colors of spring
The sky is whitening
Not many stars are left
The fragment of moon is going out
But your face in the early light
Glitters
Now we must separate

After all the words
Nothing is eased
Turn your head I have something to add
You will remember
My skirt of green silk woven loosely
The new grass will remind you of it everywhere

Autumn Night

The dew falls, the sky is a long way up, the brimming waters
    are quiet.
On the empty mountain in the companionless night
    doubtless the wandering spirits are stirring.
Alone in the distance the ship's lantern lights up one
    motionless sail.
The new moon is moored to the sky, the sound of the beetles
    comes to an end.
The chrysanthemums have flowered, men are lulling their
    sorrows to sleep.
Step by step along the veranda, propped on my stick, I keep
    my eyes on the Great Bear.
In the distance the celestial river leads to the town.

The Body of Man

The body of man is like a flicker of lightning
existing only to return to Nothingness,
like the spring growth that shrivels in autumn.
Waste no thought on the process, for it has no purpose,
coming and going like the dew.

translated with Nguyen Ngoc Bich

Rebirth

Spring goes, and the hundred flowers.
Spring comes, and the hundred flowers.
My eyes watch things passing,
my head fills with years.
But when spring has gone, not all the flowers follow.
Last night a plum branch blossomed by my door.

translated with Nguyen Ngoc Bich

The Ideal Retreat

I will choose a place where the snakes feel safe.
All day I will love that remote country.
At times I will climb the peak of its lonely mountain
to stay and whistle until the sky grows cold.

translated with Nguyen Ngoc Bich

Autumn

Sky full of autumn
earth like crystal
news arrives from a long way off following one wild goose.
The fragrance gone from the ten-foot lotus
by the Heavenly Well.
Beech leaves
fall through the night onto the cold river,
fireflies drift by the bamboo fence.
Summer clothes are too thin.
Suddenly the distant flute stops
and I stand a long time waiting.
Where is Paradise
so that I can mount the phoenix and fly there?

translated with Nguyen Ngoc Bich

Winter

Lighted brazier
small silver pot
cup of Lofu wine to break the cold of the morning.
The snow
makes it feel colder inside the flimsy screens.
Wind lays morsels of frost on the icy pond.
Inside the curtains
inside her thoughts
a beautiful woman.
The cracks of doors and windows
all pasted over.
One shadowy wish to restore the spring world:
a plum blossom already open on the hill.

translated with Nguyen Ngoc Bich

A Woodcutter on His Way Home

Here and there little breezes stir the rushes.
At dusk the birds hurry as though they were lost.
Loaded with wood he moves slowly homeward.
He moves slowly, knowing the way.

translated with Nguyen Ngoc Bich

The Substituted Poem of Laureate Quynh

This is what the professor wrote home, listen:
Tell my wife not to get heated up.
I have got it all the way north here perfectly limp.
Down south there she had better look to her clam.
Is it still tight and winding like a gopher's burrow
or is it gaping by now like a catfish grotto?
Tell her to hang onto it even if it gives her a fight.
I will be home in a couple of days.

translated with Nguyen Ngoc Bich

Women

Tea is one, wine another, women the third:
my three follies that leave me no peace.
I shall have to give up whichever I can.
I should be able to give up tea, I think. And wine.

translated with Nguyen Ngoc Bich

I have had a companion on the road
we have journeyed shoulder to shoulder
by nature the mountains are green
by nature the water is clear
midnight has passed
this nature is not known
all I hear
is startled monkeys above the monastery

from the French version by Masumi Shibata

For years I dug in the earth
trying to discover the blue sky
deeper and deeper I tunneled
until one night
I made stones and tiles fly into the air
with no effort I broke the bone of the void

from the French version by Masumi Shibata
For an alternative translation of this poem, see page 304.

A breeze strokes the water of the spring
bringing a cool sound
the moon climbs from the peak in front
lights up the bamboo window frame
With age I have found it good
to be in the heart of the mountains
To die at the foot of a cliff –
the bones would be pure forever

from the French version by Masumi Shibata

Even the man who is happy
　glimpses something
　a hair of sound touches him

　and his heart overflows with a longing
　　he does not recognize

then it must be that he is remembering
　in a place out of reach
　shapes he has loved

　in a life before this

　the print of them still there in him waiting

　　translated with J. Moussaieff Masson

Cosmology

The goddess Lakshmi
loves to make love to Vishnu
from on top
looking down she sees in his navel
a lotus
and on it Brahma the god
but she can't bear to stop
so she puts her hand
over Vishnu's right eye
which is the sun
and night comes on
and the lotus closes
with Brahma inside

translated with J. Moussaieff Masson

I like sleeping with somebody
   different

often

it's nicest when my husband is
   in a foreign country

   and there's rain in the streets at night
   and wind

   and nobody

    translated with J. Moussaieff Masson

Between his hands
Krishna takes
Yasodhā's breast
in his mouth takes
her nipple
at once he remembers
in an earlier life taking
to his mouth the conch shell
to call to battle
all bow down now to
the thought of his skin
at that moment

translated with J. Moussaieff Masson

Water pouring from clouds
in the night
of palm forests
large ears motionless
they listen
the elephants
eyes half-closed
to the sound of the heavy rain
their trunks resting on their tusks

translated with J. Moussaieff Masson

from *Kavikanthabharana*

A poet should learn with his eyes
the forms of leaves
he should know how to make
people laugh when they are together
he should get to see
what they are really like
he should know about oceans and mountains
in themselves
and the sun and the moon and the stars
his mind should enter into the seasons
he should go
among many people
in many places
and learn their languages

translated with J. Moussaieff Masson

Hiding in the
cucumber garden
simple country girl shivers
with desire
her lover on a low cot
lies tired with love
she melts into his body
with joy
his neck tight in her arms
one of her feet
flicking a necklace of
seashells hanging
on a vine
on the fence
rattles them to scare off
foxes there in the dark

translated with J. Moussaieff Masson

My husband
before leaving on a journey
is still in the house speaking
to the gods and already
separation is climbing like
bad monkeys to the windows

translated with J. Moussaieff Masson

A long time back
when we were first in love
our bodies were always as one
later you became
my dearest
and I became your dearest
alas
and now beloved lord
you are my husband
I am your wife
our hearts must be
as hard as the middle of thunder
now what have I to live for

translated with J. Moussaieff Masson

That moon which the sky never saw
    even in dreams
    has risen again

    bringing a fire
    that no water can drown

See here where the body
    has its house
    and see here my soul

    the cup of love has made the one
    drunk
    and the other a ruin

When the tavern keeper
    became my heart's companion

    love turned my blood
    to wine
    and my heart burned on a spit

When the eye is full of him
    a voice resounds

    Oh cup
    be praised
    oh wine be proud

Suddenly when my heart saw
the ocean of love

it leapt away from me calling
Look for me

The face of Shams-ud Din
the glory of Tabriz

is the sun that hearts follow
like clouds

translated with Talat Halman

When the heart bursts into flame
  it swallows up
  the believers and the faithless together

  when the bird of truth
  opens its wings
  all the images fly away

The world breaks apart
  the soul is flooded

  the pearl that dissolves into water
  is embraced by the water
  and reborn from the water

The secret appears
  and the forms of the world
  fall away

  suddenly one wave
  is flung upward
  all the way to the green dome of the sky

One moment it's a pen
  one moment it's paper
  one moment it's rapture

the soul learns to hate
good and evil
and keeps stabbing at both

Every soul that reaches God
    enters the majestic
    secret

    turns from a snake
    into a fish

    leaves solid earth
    dives into the sea
    swims in the river of Paradise

The soul moves from earthly bondage
    to the kingdom without place

    after that wherever it falls
    it is bathed in a sea of sweet odor

Absence is also
    divine poverty

    it guides the stars

    the Emperor
    turns to dust on its doorstep
    knocking

Let the glittering surface
  go out
  so that the light within
  can wake

  out of the burning sun
  light comes to the heart
  to illumine the universe

You are in the service
  of the beloved
  why are you hiding

  you are gold
  finer and brighter
  at each stroke of the hammer

It is the heart
  that sings these words
  the wine of eternity
  has made it drunk

  but these are nothing
  to the words it would sing
  if it held its breath

  translated with Talat Halman

Wise teacher tell me
　　who or what do I look like

one minute I'm a phantom
　　the next I call to the spirits

I stand unscorched and unshriveled
　　in the flames of longing
　　and I am the candle that gives light to everything

I am the smoke and the light I am one
　　and I am scattered

The one thing I ever twist in anger
　　is the peg of the heart's lyre

the one thing I ever pluck
　　with the plectrum
　　is the harp of joy

I am like milk and honey
　　I strike myself again and again
　　I stop myself

when I run mad I rattle my chains

Teacher tell me what kind
　　of bird am I
　　neither partridge nor hawk

I'm neither beautiful nor ugly
   neither this nor that

I'm neither the peddler in the market
   nor the nightingale
   in the rose garden

Teacher give me a name so that I'll know
   what to call myself

I'm neither slave nor free neither candle
   nor iron

I've not fallen in love with anyone
   nor is anyone in love with me

Whether I'm sinful or good
   sin and goodness come from another
   not from me

Wherever He drags me I go
   with no say in the matter

   translated with Talat Halman

Love you alone have been with us
   since before the beginning of the world

tell us all the secrets one by one
   we are of the same Household as you

In dread of your fire we closed our mouths
   and gave up words

but you are not fire
   you are without flames

Moment by moment
   you destroy the city of the mind

gust of wind to the mind's candle
   wine for the fire-worshipers

Friend with friends
   enemy with enemies

or somewhere between the two
   looking for both

To the sane
   the words of lovers are nothing but stories

if that was all you were
how could you turn night into day

You whose beauty sends the world reeling
your love brings about all this confusion

You are that love's masterpiece
you make it clear

O sun of God
sultan of sultans
glory and joy of Tabriz

you give light to those on earth
beauty and splendor of the age

translated with Talat Halman

If you're not going to sleep
  sit up
  I've already slept

go on and tell your story
  I've finished mine

I've finished that story
  because I'm tired

lurching the way drunks do
  staggering
  ready to pass out

Asleep or awake
  I'm thirsty
  for the beloved

my companion
  my cherished friend
  is the image
  of the beloved

Like the mirror
  I exist only because
  of that face

for whose sake
   I display features
   or hide them

When the image of the beloved smiles
   I smile
   when the image stirs and rages with passion

I stir and rage too
   with passion
   I too let go

For the rest
   why don't you
   tell it
   you

each of the pearls
   after all
   that I'm piercing and stringing together

came out of your sea

translated with Talat Halman

Tatar Songs

I

The sun rises going the rounds
as though it were tied to the apple tree.
One day if we live we will be back
making the rounds like the sun.

II

Little finger painted with henna, little copper fingernail, dice
    of gold,
is it possible to leave a lover in this world?

Because of the orchard the sun does not pass my window.
As for me I have turned yellow, shriveled by love.

Do not whiten the rooftree of the low house.
I am alone, I am unhappy, do not be cruel to me.

Why do you look out the door all the time?
I would give my life for the darkness of your eyes.

The child of the *bai* drinks water from a golden cup.
Under the moon a cloud, the moon's child.
And I, I have turned yellow, withered by love.

III

My beloved, the face is covered with blood.
The falcon's face, covered with blood.
The wind blew, a curl of hair came loose.
A wick took it, and the face covered with blood.

I built a house and it was a mirage.
But it was a shelter for my whole life.
The point of my stick was not solid
and our night had its danger.

I am dying because I always watched the road.
I looked to right and to left.
Neither you nor I will ever be done
watching the road, watching the road.

The seas turn into horses
and cupbearers.
I drank to quiet my sorrow
but it grew wilder all the time.

The whole universe is full of God
   yet His truth is seen by no one
   you have to look for Him in yourself
   you and He are not separate you are one

The other world is what can't be seen
   here on earth we must live as well as we can
   exile is grieving and anguish
   no one comes back who has once gone

Come let us be friends this one time
   let life be our friend
   let us be lovers of each other
   the earth will be left to no one

You know what Yunus is saying
   its meaning is in the ear of your heart
   we should all live truly here
   for we will not live here forever

translated with Talat Halman

Ghazal v

The drop dies in the river
of its joy
pain goes so far it cures itself

in the spring after the heavy rain the cloud
disappears
that was nothing but tears

in the spring the mirror turns green
holding a miracle
Change the shining wind

the rose led us to our eyes

let whatever is be open

translated with Aijaz Ahmad

Ghazal XII

I am not a flower of song
   nor any of the bright shuttles of music
I am the sound of my own breaking

You think of how your hair looks
I think of the ends of things

We think we know our own minds
but our hearts are children

Now that you have appeared to me I bow
may you be blessed

You look after the wretched
no wonder you came
   looking for me

translated with Aijaz Ahmad

Ghazal xv

Almost none
of the beautiful faces
come back to be glimpsed for an instant in some flower

once the dust owns them

The three Daughters of the Bier
as becomes stars
hide in the light till day has gone

then they step forth naked
but their minds are the black night

He is the lord of sleep
lord of peace
lord of night

on whose arm your hair is lying

translated with Aijaz Ahmad

Ghazal XXI

Red poppy
    a heart
    an eye

    one dewdrop on it
    a tear

    there to hide something

    she is cruel
    it leaves its mark

But the scar of the burnt heart
    oh my cry
    is nothing

    beside you oh my cry
    dove
    turned to ashes
    nightingale
    prison of color

No blaze of meeting
    could have burned like the longing to meet

the spirits were consumed
the heart suffered torture

If a man claims to be a prisoner of love
   he is a prisoner of something
   hand held down by a stone
   faithful

Oh sun
   you light the whole world
   here also
   shine

   a strange time has come over us
   like a shadow

translated with Aijaz Ahmad

Ghazal xxv

If it ever occurs to her to be kind to me
   she remembers how cruel she's been
   and it frightens her off

Her temper's as short as my tale of love is long
   much too long
   bores even the messenger

   and I despair
   and lose the thread of my own thoughts

   and can't bear to think of someone else
   setting eyes on her

translated with Aijaz Ahmad

Ghazal xxxiv

He's going around with your letter
showing
would be happy to read it out

Kind as she is she's made so fine
I'd be afraid to touch her
if she'd let me

Death will come whether I wait for her or not
I ask you to come whether I want you
or not

The vision
hangs before the Divine like a curtain
whose is it

Helpless with the fire of love
Ghalib
can't light it can't put it out

translated with Aijaz Ahmad

ASIAN FIGURES

Introduction to the Figures

There is an affinity that everyone must have noticed between poetry – certain kinds and moments of it – on the one hand, and such succinct forms as the proverb, the aphorism, the riddle, on the other. Poetry, on many occasions, gathers the latter under its name. But it seems to me likely that the proverb and its sisters are often poetry on their own, without the claim being made for them. In order to do more than suggest this, I would be led, no doubt, to step out onto that quicksand which is the attempt to define poetry, and I am not about to do that. It was never part of the purpose of what is in this book anyway. What I did want to do was to try to give voice and form to something that these other genres, and what I take to be poetry, share. There are qualities that they obviously have in common: an urge to finality of utterance, for example, and to be irreducible and unchangeable. The urge to brevity is not perhaps as typical of poetry as we would sometimes wish, but the urge to be self-contained, to be whole, is perhaps another form of the same thing, or can be, and it is related to the irreversibility in the words that is a mark of poetry.

A few instances, more or less at random, of family resemblance:

ART OF EATING
lesson number one
don't pick up the spoon
with the fork.

Antonio Machado

When a dog runs at you, whistle for him.

Thoreau, Journal for June 26, 1840

After the house is finished, leave it.

George Herbert – Jacula Prudentum

He whose face gives no light shall never become a star.

Blake – Proverbs of Hell

Even the smallest of creatures carries a sun in its eyes.

Antonio Porchia – Voices

And the heart
Is pleased
By one thing
After another.

Archilochus – translated by Guy Davenport

In the Figures that follow, I did not set out to prove that the material I was using was "really" poetry. It's true that I was trying to embody, or at least to indicate, particular qualities of poetry which I think that kind of material often has. But what I aimed for in each case was something that seemed to me single, irreducible, and complete in a manner plainly its own. I was not concerned with whether it was complete grammatically, for example, and the occasional ellipses of language would make it clear to me, if I had not known it, that I was more concerned with the spoken idiom (my own, that is) than the written convention. It occurs to me that this has been another perennial blood-link between this kind of material and poetry. And I wanted what makes these pieces complete (if they are) and what holds the words in their order, to be the same thing.

I do not, in case anyone wondered, know the original languages. Several years ago, Mrs. Crown, of the Asia Society in New York, gave me a number of collections of Asian proverbs, short poems, and riddles, saying that she thought I might be interested in them. They were presented, for the most part, ideogram by ideogram, with literal renderings, in the original order, and notes. It was not long before I discovered what some of my interest – the part of it that led to these Figures – was. I have relied throughout on those collections and translations – in other words, wholly on prior English versions, and the scholarship of others. My own adaptations of the material were not undertaken with a view to being – necessarily – literal, or to adding to anyone's knowledge of Asian literature as such. At the same time, I have not at any point deliberately altered the main sense of the original. It was important to me, for the purpose I've described above, that it should be just what it was – material, and anonymous – and I felt indebted to the original meaning, insofar as I could grasp it.

–W.S.M., 1973

Korean Figures

Goes all right
take the credit
goes all wrong
blame your ancestors

They steal the saint
while you're making the shrine

Kick the world
break your foot

Keeps going
ant around a sieve

Big pond
little anthole
the whole bank falls in

Pretty
but sour inside

Little sour fruits
ripe first
burst first

　　　　　　　Hard to hold out a cup
　　　　　　　farther than the heads of your
　　　　　　　　children

Your hands turn
to you first

　　　　　　　You'd think the ivy
　　　　　　　would grow forever
　　　　　　　but it has its end

Too much
for a donkey
piled on a grasshopper

　　　　　　　Even with your aunt
　　　　　　　bargain

Tree grows the way they want it to
that's the one they cut first

You've got an ax but you can't use it
the other one's got
a needle
but he can

Your own ax
bit you

Tongue swings
ax strokes

Ugly baby
the one to love
angry one
the one to hug

You give the child
you don't like
one extra

The crying baby
is the one that gets fed

Looking for it all over the place
three years
carrying it all the time like a baby

You try to sell the fur
when you've only just found
the pawmark

Just because you're family
you tell the guests what to bring

No more to say
than a borrowed sack

Three bushels of beads
don't make a string
if they haven't got a string

Can't grow it
once you roast it

Wash a bean
that's how polished
he seems

Bean seed
bean babies

Only have to have a toothache
and they give you something
to chew

Wants to cut bread
before the wheat's ripe

Got water on for beans
before the plants are up

You break the kettle
to cook the beans

I wouldn't believe you
if you said they make bean cakes
out of beans

Nothing to eat
like a bear
who licks the soles of his feet

No beard
long beard
makes no difference if you don't eat

Worth burning down the house
sometimes
for the fun of killing the bedbugs

For every beggar
a day comes
bringing a guest

All right you've nothing to
give me
don't break my bowl

Can't even beg
without clothes

The feathers come first
then flight

Blind
blames the ditch

Can't see
steal your own things

        Knows his way
        stops seeing

Blind horse
follows
bells

        Tap it
        if you're going to walk across it

Adversary
crossing on the same log

        All dressed up
        walking in the dark

Burned lips on broth
now blows on cold water

        Too hot
        no taste

Nothing to do
pray

A tailor dies
with the end of a thread
in his mouth

Picture of a cake
when you're hungry

New Year's
and nothing to eat
but the presents

Eat cakes lying down
get raisins
in your eyes

Cake in both hands
what next

Better to die
of too much

Ask the mouth
it says
cake

Candlestick in a pawnshop
can't explain

Candy today
sweeter than honey
tomorrow

Even the rich
prefer cash

Smart
a cat rolling an egg

Nobody appreciates
cats
or daughters-in-law

The rats decide
the cat ought to be belled

Believe him
when the cat swears off meat

Cries
like a rat when a cat dies

As a cat pities a rat

Charcoal
writes everybody's name
black

Gave it all away
and got
cheeks slapped

Cheeks slapped downtown
good and angry
uptown

Somebody else
knocks down the nuts
you pick them up

Withered chestnut
hangs three seasons
good chestnut falls
after one

Dog days
skinny hens
scratch in the thatch

Eats
feathers and all

Even a child
goes on hitting long enough
it starts to hurt

Listen
even to a baby

Would try to eat broth
with a fork

No rust
on a clamshell

Still alive
no cobweb
over the mouth

Cotton cloth
better than no cloth

Cow in the stream
eating from both banks

Easy
as riding
on a sleeping cow

Cow
parched by the sun
pants at the moon

Vanished
like a crab's eyes

Even sideways
if it gets you there

Quiet as
a crane watching
a hole over water

> Can't crawl
> and tries to jump

Crow
has twelve notes
none of them music

> I eat the cucumber
> my way

When he's married off three daughters
he doesn't need locks anymore

> Suffering hurts
> not death

Silver tongue
pays off
debt of gold

See one thing he does
know the rest

                           Escape from the deer
                           get caught by the tiger

Scared by
his own wind

                           Crooked
                           sees everything
                           that way

Hunchback
is good to
his parents

                           Even on dog turds
                           the dew falls

Would put horseshoes
on a dog

No good for me
too good for the dog

Ate what I gave it
then bit me

Black dog
bath
blacker

Chased a chicken
stands looking up

A dog with
two back doors

Neglect is a dog
in a dead man's house

No sleep
no dreams

Hang them up
beat them
they make a noise
if they're drums

                            Any drum
                            sets her dancing

Dumb
groans all alone
pain under his cold ribs

                            Dumb child
                            its own mother
                            doesn't know what it's
                                thinking

Stealing a bell
covers his ears

                            Good story
                            but not ten times

Hearing
is sickness
deafness cures

Hungry
his eyes
look like empty pickle jars

When the rotten egg crows

Trying to smash a wall
with eggs

Palsied
egg thief

If you shut your eyes
they'll bite off your nose

Family going to the dogs
when the eldest daughter-in-law
grows a beard

Man with ten vices
sneers at the man with one

More announcements
than dishes

Your own cold
worse than somebody else's
   pneumonia

                Each finger
                can suffer

Jumps into the fire
carrying kindling

                Fish say
                home water
                doesn't look
                like other water

Long way
to the law
fist right here

                Champion
                shadowboxer

Stingy
squeezes blood
out of fleas

No flower
stays
a flower

Flier
goes higher
than creeper
or leaper

Frog
forgets he had a tail

Leaks here
will leak somewhere else

Builds the Great Wall in one night
asleep

Reads the menu
before he goes to the wake

What he can't help at three
he'll do when he's eighty

Bald
choosing hair ribbons

Plucked hair
won't go back into
its own hole

Hammer's too light
it bounces

Wait till he's falling
then push

Wears heaven for a helmet
and shakes his head

Thinks heaven
is a penny

Even if the sky falls
there will be a little hole
to get out through

Outside
is hell

Even honey
tastes like medicine
when it's medicine

Old horse
keeps waiting
for beans

Now nobody comes
to the horse stables
but donkey owners

Finally gets
a horse
then he wants a groom

No big horse
use a little one

Everybody thinks
you had supper
at the other place

House burns down
save the nails

Knife can't whittle
its own handle

        Calls that a meal
        but the liver can't hear him

Love meets itself
coming back

        Sends the guest away
        then starts cooking

Some talk of funerals
whatever happens

        They come with the cure
        when he's buried

A man's mind changes
every hour
but love –

        I know
        my own
        pennies

Wrap up musk
twice
still smell it

        Thread has to go
        where the needle went

Needle thief
dreams
of spears

        Tries to sew
        tied up in the thread

The address
means more than the kinship

        Wise
        at the end

Not big
but a pepper

In a thousand chickens
one phoenix
hidden

        If they're the same price
        pick the prettiest

No home
water bucket
with no rope

        Scratching
        somebody else's itch

How long
is a snake in a cave

        Frost
        settling
        on snow

Quiet
like a house where the witch
has just stopped dancing

Blind fortune-teller
can't see his own
death coming

Sparrow flying
over a rice mill
keeps both eyes open

Sparrow shouts
in the teeth of death

Wren
don't run after stork
with your legs

Iron hinge
straw door

Swallow
no bigger than that
flies all the way south

A gentleman
would rather drown
than swim dog-paddle

Dress sword
and no pants

Grabbed for the head
got the tail

Day talk
birds listening
night talk
rats listening

Too tall
part empty

Learn to steal
late in life
make up for lost time

Silent
like the thief the dog bit

If the stars bring the thief
the dog won't bark

Where there's no tiger
the hares
swagger

Bent trees
watch
an ancestor's grave

You hoist me into the tree
before you shake it

Good tree
that's what the worm thought too

Tries to put both arms
in the same sleeve

Wade
as if it were deep

Crooked
as walnut meat

Get rid of one wart
end up with two

                    Pour it on the head
                    it ends up on the heels

Saved him from drowning
now he wants his bundles

                    Poor man
                    drowned
                    nothing floated but the purse

Water follows
a water leader

                    Has to drink the whole sea
                    to learn what it tastes like

Wails all night
without finding out who's dead

                    Just sink
                    one well
                    deep enough

Widow
knows what a widow
is crying about

If it costs the same
lodge with a widow

Too little wine
with tears in it

Words
have no feet
but they get there

Can't pick up a word again
like an arrow

Even a worm
goes
its own way

You strike a better bargain
if you're not hungry

Can clench all right
but can't open

Dove in a tree
but his mind
in a bean field

Gone like an egg in a river

Beauty
costs

Beauty
depends on the glasses

Buried diamond
is still a diamond

Man with twelve arts
but can't cook his supper

Chase two hares
both get away

No hares left to hunt
he boils his hound

          Cock silent
          hen sings
          luckless sunrise
          death listening

To know
is to be sick

          Dead leaf
          tells pine needle
          hush

He's the cripple
not his legs

          Love deprives him
          of all four limbs
          all five

Blames his mirror

So worked up
lucky he has two nostrils

        Invited nowhere
        goes everywhere

Sees a horse
needs to ride

        Nothing to me
        and far away

Nobody notices hunger
but nobody misses dirt

        Every grave
        holds a reason

Burmese Figures

Pound bran all you please
never get rice that way

          Can't sharpen it
          once it's rotten

One of the dreams
of the dumb

          Disease unknown
          cure unknown

No trees
so a bush rules

          Do it wrong
          do it twice

Blind
not afraid
of seeing ghosts

Doesn't know whether
he's on a stallion or a mare

Keeps moving
doesn't know this place
either

Worse knowing nothing
than having nothing

Telling a fish
about water

Day won't come
to the hen's cackle

Laughs when
somebody else does it

The seven shameless creatures
tell their names

Carries a harp
he can't play

Only cotton
and thinks it can stand
any comparison

No rice
manage with beans
no brains
join the army

Eats all he wants
then upsets the dish

I brought up this monkey
now he
makes faces at me

When you've died once
you know how

Can't beat the big boys
bullies the little girls

Too scared
to be responsible

Clenches his fist
in his underpants

Comes from hell
you can't scare him with ashes

Man unlike sugarcane
only sweet sometimes

Harelipped couple
blowing on their fire

Thorn falls
hole in the leaf
leaf falls
hole in the leaf

Lady Unluck
has the rain
for her train

At first the hare
was in front

Even when he's praying
keep an eye
on his hands

                        Thief shouting
                        man man

Too dirty to eat
too tempting to throw away

                        When I farm the rain fails
                        when I steal the dogs bark

It was when we were winning
that the oar broke

                        Try to put out a fire
                        brings on the wind

Saved it
for the maggots

Japanese Figures 1

Nations die
rivers go on
mountains
go on

          Everywhere
          birds make
          that song

Most beautiful
just before

          Autumn rides down
          on one leaf

Autumn
the deer's
own color

          Ice comes from water
          but can teach it
          about cold

If you're going to be a dog
be a rich man's dog

                          Stop
                          under a big tree

Nobody
keeps the months or the days
from their travels

                          Snow on my grass hat
                          weighs lightly
                          when I think of it as my own

The world turns
through partings

                          Flute blows
                          autumn comes
                          with its deer like hopeless lovers

Loves even
the crow on her roof

Star
watching
the day break

Doesn't dress up his teeth in silk

He's hard
as his bones

So beautiful
took away
my eyes

Makes his own
rust

Far
from his own ears

If a nail sticks up
the hammer comes

Got no clothes
can't lose your shirt

Sudden
like a spear from a window

Crow
tried to be cormorant
drowned

Caution
takes no castles

Fish
dance all you like
but stay in the river

Polishing
won't make it a diamond

His hundred days' sermons
all gone in one fart

Feet of the lantern bearer
move in the dark

Skillful hand
but can't hold water

        Foot itches
        he scratches the shoe

Blind man
peeping through a fence

        Can stand pain
        even three years
        if it's somebody else's

Hangs up a sheep's head
but sells dog meat

        One dog barks at nothing
        ten thousand others
        pass it on

Business
or other screen
has to be crooked to stand up

Thief
plans even his naps

Word gets away
four fast horses
can't catch it

The mouth
is one gate
of hell

Autumn
sky changes
seven and a half times

Better than the holiday
is the day before

Departs once
is forgotten day
after day

See what her
mother looks like

Bad wife
sixty years
of poor harvests

A child
ties you by the neck
to the three worlds

Spits straight up
learns something

Good luck
bad luck
twisted into one rope

What is coming
is uncertainty

Destiny
even swings
the sleeves

Some places that were mulberry fields
are now the sea

Heaven
is a coarse net
but nothing gets through

Rich
even strangers visit
poor
even family stays away

So close
to each other
they would hold water

See more
by the poor man's
one lantern

Many blind men
following
one blind man

Tries to catch the moon
as it floats by

Heaven
is sleep

Running away
doesn't stop to read signposts

Caught the thief
found I was
his father

Sardine threatens
who knows it

Can't reach
where it itches

If you tried to sell it
they'd think you stole it

When he talks
it clouds the tea

Singing
that stirred the dust on the beams

Full of danger
as an egg pyramid

Bell cricket
caged for singing

Summer rain
so hard
parted the horse's mane

Blind man
calling his
lost staff

Warm it for ten days
cools off in one

Age comes by itself
but not learning

The traitor
has the best
patriot costume

Takes up
the old handle

Sparrows a hundred years old
still dance
the sparrow dance

Sickly
survives them all

Even a thief
needs an apprenticeship

One trouble goes
to make room for another

Repentance
never goes first

The mummy hunter
turns mummy

Just got it
in time to lose it

Poor
as the dead

We meet
to part

The labor of the poor
makes the hills higher

Tomorrow's wind
blows
tomorrow

Never mind
what they say
go see

Crooked branch
crooked shadow

Thirty-six plans
the best of them
flight

Acorns arguing
which is tallest

Run out of wisdom
start boasting

Ocean
doesn't fuss
about the streams

Prefer one day here
to a thousand hereafter

One inch ahead
the whole world
is dark

Coffin bearers
pray
for a plague year

Many years
many shames

Talk about tomorrow
the rats
will laugh

Bird shadow
crosses door
guests coming

If it happened
it will happen
again

If he flatters you
watch him

Philippine Figures

Coconut
has the moon inside

           Little hollows
           climbing coconut trunk forever
           Adam's footprints

Squash plant
child sits waiting
mother goes on climbing

           Corn
           hides in a cloak
           but his beard shows

Tobacco
no one too great
to kiss its leaves

           Dry leaf
           flutters down swearing
           never to come back

Ant
back
after back

Bat flies like a handkerchief
lands like
a sack

Centipede on the wall
the Virgin's comb

Crab waves
but then doesn't wait

Earthworm
little string
through a mountain

Fly
eats with the best

Grandfather cat
old as he is
never had a bath

Any weather
chicken's
pants are rolled up

                              Rooster
                              torch in front
                              fishing pole behind

The house of the Virgin
is an egg
no stairs no door

                              Parrot never sinned has no debts
                              speaks like a Christian
                              but they put him in a cage

Sow walks
and the babies sing

                              The ears are brothers
                              but never see each other

Ear's tame enough to be touched
but won't stay to be looked at

Fingers
ten brothers
with white hats

Tongue
pale pig
in a bone fence

Footsteps
I'll follow you
then you follow me

Hunchback
never gets paid
for carrying that thing all the time

The rain is St. Joseph's canes
can't count them can't touch them
none of them is the last

Water
needs no feet
heals itself

Stars
sown at dusk
reaped at dawn

St. Anne
lives in the sun
nobody can look at her house

Bamboo floor
many brothers
lying face down

Who looks at a mirror
to see a mirror

Pillow
ate only once
since it was born

Church bell
goes on calling
no one comes

Coffin boat
pilot asleep
sailing

Guitar only cries
when you pick it up

Japanese Figures 11

Thinks even her acne
is dimples

                Autumn
                glass sky
                horses fattening

Bird flies up
where your foot was going

                Skin in the morning
                bone by nightfall

Touch it
like a bruise

                Luck turns
                wait

To the winners
the losers
were rebels

Never mind
it's across the river

Pleasure flower
pain seed

Start to speak
lips feel the cold autumn wind

While folly parades
wisdom stands aside

No one has less
than seven
habits

A debt
you have it
because you haven't got it

Whole place no bigger
than a cat's forehead

She
changes
like a cat's eyes

                                  Helps more than the cat

The news
wakes you
like water poured into your ear

                                  Wake up
                                  as much as you can

Drops of water
from a balcony

                                  Nobody bothers
                                  the bad boys

Can't tell what God's
going to do next

                                  Only wear
                                  the one pair
                                  of straw shoes at a time

Get there first
and then argue

Don't bother God
God won't bother you

Can't use your belly
for your back

Shirt's pretty near
but skin's
nearer

Do it hard enough
you'll do it

All those good deeds
some day you're bound
to get rich

Once I'm right
I'll fight anybody

Reads a lot
he doesn't understand

Seed hardly sprouted
you know it's sandalwood

Eat first
poetry later

Smart hawk
covers his claws

Get on
have to stay on

Get out of the game
to watch it

Get three women together
that's noise

Too big
to be bright all through

Just didn't get there in time
so he killed himself
without you

               Daddy
               started you right

They think their own
is the smart one

               Keeps counting up
               the dead child's
               age

Death
collects all the tongues

               Worm
               gets at lion
               from inside

Save me from a small mind
when it's got nothing to do

Sleeves touch
because they were going to
since the world began

Live there long enough
for you it becomes
the center of the kingdom

One god goes
but another comes

Travelers
get away with anything

Jelly
in a vise

They call a bat a bird
they have no birds

Ask him
he's careful
let him tell it himself

Ask
ashamed for a minute
don't ask don't know
ashamed forever

Clouds fly into the moon
wind full of blossoms

As like
as moon and turtle shell

As like
as clouds and mud

Thief
used the moonlight
and got away in it

Burns his fingernails
to save candles

Kills an ox
trying to straighten its horns

Marry
your own size

Praying
to a horse's ears

Serpent lives
one thousand years in the sea
one thousand years in the mountain
comes out dragon

Owe more to the one who
brought you up
than to the one who bore you

If the fish are going to be heartless
the water's heartless too

If it's good
hurry

Chinese Figures I

One lifetime in office
the next seven lives a beggar

A judge decides for ten reasons
nine of which nobody knows

If you get in a fight with a tiger
call your brother

Every house
has its black pig

Don't curse your wife
at bedtime

Big thunder
little rain

The peddler won't tell you
that his melons are bitter

A man can't walk an inch
without the help of heaven

Three feet above you
the spirits

You can whitewash a crow
but it won't last

It's hard to dismount
from a tiger

Before you beat a dog
find out whose he is

One dog steals
and another gets punished

The hissing starts
in the free seats

Out of ten fingers
nine are different

For a whole day
he does nothing
like the immortals

In the first half of the night
ponder your own faults
in the second half those of others

Eggs
if they're wise
don't fight with stones

If two men feed a horse
it will stay thin

Truth is
what the rich say

The rich
are never
as ugly

One foot
on each boat

Melon on a housetop
has two choices

                                        When the heart dies
                                        you can't even
                                        grieve

Lives one day
what does it know
of the seasons

                                        Shines with its own
                                        sun and moon

Even from those we think lovely
animals run away

                                        Straightened too much
                                        crooked as ever

Borrows the flowers
for the shrine

Enough mosquitoes
sound like thunder

Who could like listening
to good advice

One be one side of the blade
one be the other
together cut through metals

Cows run with the wind
horses against it

All your labors
flowing east in the rivers

Hollow mountain
listens to everything

Wild swan print
in the snow

Thunders before
you can stop your ears

When he draws a tiger
it's a dog

Afraid not to get it
then afraid to lose it

If you can't smile
don't open a shop

Don't judge a man
till his coffin's closed

Drops his sword in the river
marks the boat
to show where

All he knows of the leopard
is one spot

Dreamed that his pen
blossomed

Gone like today's flower
tomorrow

Eye can't see
its own lashes

Drank a shadow
thought it was a snake
got snake-swallowing sickness

So many lice
he's stopped itching

Treats the people
as carefully
as a sore

Sun gets there so seldom
the dogs bark at it

You gone
every day is like three autumns

Anxious heart
flutters like a flag

Ants on a millstone
whichever way they walk
they go around with it

Malay Figures

Slow splashing splashing
wakes me
and I cling to the wet pillow

                    Stepping on a long thorn
                    to me the sight of her hair

Little lights in the orchard
and she is hung with pieces of glass
and I am near death because she
    looked at me

                    Why do you pretend to light
                      the empty lantern
                    why do you pretend
                    that there is a flame in you

I thought my soul was dead
and you found it was a box of sweet basil

Some wear bracelets on their wrists
I wear them on my ankles
and go my own way in love

                I see wind far away in flags
                my heart is not patient
                sick with waiting

The deer lies for a long time with a
    broken leg
and nobody finds it
the whole mountain's been on fire for
    seven years
and you've just noticed

                Nails dyed with henna
                fragrance of poured rose water
                you were my sickness and you
                    are my cure

I have survived seven days in the
    wilderness
without food or water
but one day without you and there is
    little left of me

Moonlight falls on piled fruit
this grief is like no one else's
there are crowds here all the time but I
   am alone

                  Ferns bend into the water
                  over there egrets are flying
                  I sit helpless with longing

Oh temple flower
blooming in the dragon's mouth

                  Everywhere jewels have fallen
                  love is the dew
                  at daybreak

Moonlit backwater
it is an Egyptian prince weaving
but the light in my eyes is you

                  On the soft shore the clams
                      bake in the sun
                  as the Prophet loved his
                      people I love you

I would die
of your fingers
if I could be buried in your palm

         The great flocks of green
            pigeons may not come back
         but he is like my shroud
         which may rot but will never
            be changed

If you go upriver pick me a flower
if you die before me wait
just beyond the grave

         Daybreak with clouds flying
            and one star
         like a knife in the hill
         if I could find her I would see
            nothing else

Unless she is the one
sail on to death
like an empty ship

The fish line goes out
and out
but one end is in my hand

It's only where pretty girls live
that he thinks his lost hen
might be found

Let us row over to the fort crusted
    with seashells
even priests sin in spite of their
    learning
and what do we know

Some squirrels jump higher
        than others
but sooner or later they
come down

Everything by the book
and you talk about love
too easily

You knew what I was like
and you started it

The straits are like a new country
there is nothing in my eyes
and a hole in my heart

           The lime tree bends to the
              still water
           how sweet your voice is
           when you are thinking of
              another

The palm tree is tall smoke is taller
Mount Ophir is taller
above them all is the desire of my
    heart

           The lighthouse
           reveals the low mangroves of
              the shore
           you give me hope and the sky
              comes back from far away

Rough water drowns the gosling
money drives out manners
poverty drives out reason

I'm tired of planting rice in pine
    country
I've sown the seeds of kindness again
    and again
but gold is all they care for

            Neither rice nor kindness
            will bear a crop here

If you know a song
sing it

            Setting out for the island
            forget all your clothes
            but not me

Chinese Figures II

Old man
the sun leaving
the mountain

                             Nobody believes
                             the old

Ten women
nine of them
jealous

                             Over a good man
                             a flame three feet high
                             stands guard

Where he walks
the grass stops growing

                             Ten bald men
                             nine tell lies
                             the tenth says nothing

The bald tell lies
the blind are as bad as they can be
but the one-eyed are worse

                Cat-headed man
                with rat's eyes

Can't wait
till it's cooked

                Can't be an old family
                no old pictures in the hall

Can't put out a fire
from a distance

                Rich man
                turns poor
                starts to teach

No use trotting out your courtesies
before the military

Too polite
to be telling the truth

Don't invite women
they bring their children

Careful
ties his hat on

Even by moonlight
if you're alone
carry a red lantern

When you're finished
go home

Leave a bit of tail
on account of the flies

Use each coin
on both sides

If you hand over the bow
you hand over the arrow

Prefer one who knows how
to three
who don't

Rat runs off with a squash
holding it
by the little end

Your relatives can find you
by the sound of your money

Most eyes will open
to look at money

Even heroism
can be bought

Hats of honor
never forget
how to fly

You have money
anybody can teach you
to count

Fat horse
feeds at night

Making money
is digging
with a needle

See three days ahead
be rich for thousands of years

Rank and position
gulls on water

Find a gold ring in the noodles
lose it in the bath

When they want to learn
what he's like
they make him rich

The rich
have relatives
for miles

Honor
is brought
by servants

Wear rags
and the dogs bite

When you're poor
nobody believes you

Too poor
to keep rats

One rat turd
ruins the rice

Has to beat the drum
and row too
busy

Think of evil
as hot water
with your hand in it

Can't have two points
on one needle

Wanted to know
where the sun went down
died looking

Let your children
taste a little cold
and a little hunger

While they talk together
a thousand hills
rise between them

As long as your pot's boiling
friends
happen to be passing

Scruples
lead you
to hunger

The door marked Good
sticks

Flattery comes
from below

Where money goes
flattery follows

Sits in the hole
of a coin
and hangs on

Some steal when it rains
who don't when it snows

Can't keep heaven
on a rope

Hell has no door
everyone makes
his own

The back of pleasure
is pain

After winning
comes losing

In time the gambler
sells

A name
like a drum
on a hill

Even the bugs
are trying to run
from death

Life
candleflame
wind coming

So many die with dark hair
it's good to see it gray

We are birds in a wood
the great end comes there
and each flies on his way

Death is standing
on his eyebrows

Burnt tortoise
the pain
stays inside

Desperation sends
the man to the noose
the dog over the wall

Rat climbs an ox horn
narrower
and narrower

Blind rider blind horse
midnight big ditch

Cold water
dripping
into the heart

His eyes are blind
and they hurt anyway

The flea bites
and the louse is punished

Earth tea better
than hell soup

Asking questions
beats wit

Even from fools
the wise learn

One word
can warm
the three months of winter

One stroke of the saw
and the gourd is two ladles

Books don't empty words
words don't empty thoughts

Easier to cut off a head
than to shut a mouth

Secrets on earth
thunder in heaven

Winning a case
costs too much

If you want to blame
you'll blame

Don't insult
those in office
cheat them

In office
you can save more
than you earn

The wind got up in the night
and took our plans away

So cold
the cocks crow at midnight

Lao Figures

Says yes
when nobody asked

                Outside the ways of the old
                the ghosts

When luck comes
keep
your head

                The more you want to own
                the more you die

Close to death
you see how tender
the grass is

                High up
                where nobody likes him

Chinese Figures III

Seventh month
sharpens the mosquito's mouth

        The little snow stops the plows
        the big snow stops the riverboats

Set out in an evening
of mist

        Long ago famous for learning
        now nothing but a common
        god in a village

Old peasant sees statue
asks how
did it grow

        Old peasant sees stiltwalker
        says half of him
        isn't human

Old man's harvest
brought home in one hand

Just because you're cured
don't think you'll live

If it's dirty work
borrow the tools

O locusts
just eat
the neighbors' fields

Tell a man
that you'd thought him much younger
and that his clothes look expensive

Poisons himself
to poison the tiger

In every family
something's the matter

That isn't a man
it's a bean on a straw

A liar
an egg in midair

Poisons him
and charges him for it

Don't tease
a nine-tailed fox

Rat falls
into the flour jar
white eyes rolling

Too stingy
to open his eyes

Wheat found for nothing
and the devil the miller

He'll grow up to be a clown
third class

Even the gods lose
when they gamble

                    Heart like fifteen water buckets
                    seven rising
                    eight going down

Write a bad dream
on a south wall
the sun will turn it into a promise

SUN AT MIDNIGHT

Poems by Musō Soseki

Introduction to Musō

Everything that remains to our world of the many talents of the man known to us as Musō Soseki is addressed to our most intimate nature, and yet we approach him now, from wherever we are, over vast distances.

He was born ten years after Dante, in 1275 according to our reckoning, which was not the reckoning in his birthplace in the province of Ise, on the coast far to the west of the capital of Japan, then named Edo. The forested province of Ise had been the home for over a thousand years of one of the most revered shrines of Shinto, the one that houses the legendary mirror of the sun goddess Amaterasu, a mythological ancestor of the emperor. The shrine itself and the compound are, as they were when Musō was born, a celebrated example of a pure form of Japanese architecture known as the Divine Style – plain, archaic, severe, and elegant, its origins linked to the worship of trees and the building of ships, and to the defining of enclosed clearings in the forest in order to establish, with a ritual use of space, gardens.

This practice, and the legends that emanated from it, must have been part of the familiar world around Musō in his first years. He may have been taken to the great shrine as an infant. Certainly he saw, then or later, others built on the same pattern, and the images they presented to him would have made a deep impression on a child who was to become one of the great garden designers of Japan.

But his parents were Buddhists, his mother a devout worshiper of the Bodhisattva Avalokiteshvara, the representation of compassion. The tradition of medieval Buddhist hagiography is stiff with conventions, as other hagiographical traditions are, and some of its accounts are legends. A few that came to embroider what was remembered of the life of Musō seem familiar, like recurrent dreams. It was told that Musō's mother had prayed to Avalokiteshvara for a child, and had dreamed one night of a golden light flowing into her mouth. It was a full thirteen months later, however, before Musō was born.

His third year, according to the history, was one of loss. His family moved away from Ise to the province of Kai, and in August of that year his mother died. Those familiar with the life and writings of Dōgen Zenji (1200–1253) will recall that Dōgen's mother died when Dōgen was eight years old, and that her death – and the sight of the smoke of the incense burning beside her body – became the first recognizable step toward his own religious realization. Dōgen had lost his father at the age of three. There is a tradition in Zen, and in Buddhism in general, of children who were foundlings, or orphans, or who were given up to temples at a very early age, and Musō combined these. During the year after the death of his mother he is said to have shown a precocious religious fervor, reciting sutras and prayers before the Buddhist images. A religious life was predicted for him and then probably was expected of him. He was a particularly gentle child who avoided arguments and shunned contention of any kind, even rough games with children of his own age. When he was nine his father took him to the Shingon temple in Kai and gave him up to the religious life.

There Musō became a student of Mantrayāna Buddhism, returning only on occasional visits to see his father and stepmother. She cooked sumptuous meals to celebrate his being at home, and when he went back to the temple he took some of her delicious food with him to share with his friends, who probably subsisted most of the time on rice and tea. So she invited him to bring his friends home with him. One day he saw someone nearby eating a rich dinner while his servants ate almost nothing, and he resolved that if ever he had servants, their food would not differ from his own.

At eighteen he went to Nara to take his vows as a monk and have his head shaved. After that he devoted himself entirely to the study of Buddhist texts, until one day he was present at the death, in great anguish of spirit, of a learned Buddhist, who had been a noted authority of esoteric Buddhism and Tendai metaphysics, and had preached for years on Buddhist doctrine. Musō was shaken to see that all this man had known about Buddhism had helped him so little at the moment of his death. He had heard of a school of Buddhism that was based upon a "special transmission outside the scriptures" and he determined to learn about it. When he was not yet twenty he left the Shingon sect and became a student of Zen at Ken'nin-ji in Kyoto, and then at Engaku-ji and Kenchō-ji in Kamakura.

The director of Kenchō-ji was a Chinese monk named Issan who had recently arrived (1299) in Japan to escape the Mongol occupation of China. He became Musō's teacher, and Musō remained with him, practicing fervently, for a number of years. As he did, his doubt, his anxiety at his own lack of realization and clarity, grew until one day in desperation he said to Issan, "I cannot attain enlightenment. Show it to me."

Issan said, "There is no word in our school. There is no rule to transmit."

"Show me your compassion and your way."

"There is no compassion. And there is not any way."

Musō decided that there was no point in remaining with Issan and he went to the nearby temple of Engaku-ji. Master Kōhō-Ken'nichi there, a pupil at one time of another Chinese master, was famous for his insight. Musō went to see him and repeated his final conversation with Issan to Kōhō, who answered, "You should have said to Issan, 'Teacher, you have revealed too much.'" At these words Musō is said to have had a faint glimpse of the realization he was seeking, but he knew it was no more than that. He set out on a pilgrimage to the north. He spent the summer of 1305, his thirtieth year, in Zen practice in a hermitage in the province of Jōshū. One night he sat out in the garden where there was a cool breeze. Very late, he rose to go back into the hermitage. He had no light, but the place was so familiar that he thought he knew exactly where he was, and he reached out to steady himself against a wall. But the wall wan not there and he fell. Suddenly he burst out laughing, for he felt the anguish and intense searching of so many years suddenly dissolved. He wrote his *tōki-no-ge*, or satori poem, and in the autumn took it to Kōhō, who questioned him and gave the seal of his approval to Musō's realization. Musō remained with Kōhō, and three years later Kōhō transmitted to him his own dead master's robe, making Musō his successor.

But Musō was not drawn to the courtly and hierarchical world of official Zen. He left Kamakura and spent most of the next twenty years in remote temples and hermitages in the provinces, practicing Zen to clarify and deepen his insight. Yet despite his avoidance of the centers of fashion and influence, his reputation grew, and in 1325 Emperor Go-Daigo appointed Musō to the temple of Nanzen-ji in Kyoto, one of the most important and revered Zen temples in Japan, and there the emperor himself became a student of Musō. In 1329 the shogun appointed him to the temple of Engaku-ji, and Musō returned to Kamakura.

Japan at the time was torn by civil wars. The imperial power had eroded and passed into the hands of the warlords of Kamakura. Emperor Go-Daigo was anxious to regain the lost power of the throne, and the result was a series of fierce and devastating campaigns. In 1334 the emperor brought Musō back from Kamakura to Nanzen-ji. But in the following years the warrior lords rose to power and the emperor took refuge in a temple on Mount Hiei. Musō retired from his position at Nanzen-ji and took up residence at the smaller temple of Rin-sen-ji, by the Ōi River on the west of Kyoto. In June of 1336 Ashikaga Takauji entered Kyoto in triumph and became the first of the Ashikaga dynasty, which was to endure through fifteen generations, during almost two and a half centuries.

Musō was already known to the new ruler, who was himself

a dedicated student of Buddhism. Takauji and his brother, Tadayoshi, both had consulted Musō on religious matters, and they continued to do so once they were in power. Takauji's written questions to Musō, and Musō's replies, were later assembled and edited by one of Musō's successors to form the volume known as *Muchū Mondō, Dialogues in the Dream.* Takauji, like Musō's mother, was particularly devoted to the veneration of the bodhisattva of compassion, Avalokiteshvara. Not at ease in the world of power and conflict, he cherished a wish to retire from it altogether, and two years after his triumphal entry into Kyoto he turned over his duties to his brother Tadayoshi and devoted himself to the study of the Buddha dharma.

Takauji was tormented by the thought of the many who had suffered and died because of the civil wars in which he had played so important a part. At Musō's suggestions he founded Ankoku-ji, "temples of peace," and his brother built Rishō-tō, a Buddhist stūpa.

The wave of temple building brought into play some of Musō's own talents. In his midsixties, in 1339, he was consulted in the restoration of the temple of Saihō-ji and its garden in the western part of Kyoto. The original temple had been built 600 years earlier by a Buddhist monk, and at one time many buildings had occupied the site, but the entire temple had been destroyed during one of the periods of civil wars that had ravaged Japan.

The patron of the restored Saihō-ji and its garden was a nobleman named Nakahara no Chikahide, and the garden that Musō designed for the temple became famous in the history of Japanese gardens and of Japanese Buddhism.

In Japan gardens and religious observance had been closely associated for a very long time, and the boundary between architecture and gardens was indefinite. The formal compound of a Shinto temple, its ground covered with pebbles, is at once part of the enclosed structure surrounding the sacred tree and a garden, an ancestor of the raked-gravel gardens of the Zen tradition. The art of gardening had assumed as natural a role in Japanese religious custom as the arts of painting and sculpture, architecture and chant. It was not conceived of simply as a decorative addition to a place of human use. In the settings of Shinto and of Japanese Buddhism it suggests, and is meant to exemplify, a view of being.

The gardens of the Pure Land sect of Buddhism, which had been established in Japan almost three centuries before Musō's birth, were intended to evoke the paradise of Amida (Amitābha) Buddha, the Buddha of the setting sun and the hereafter. The veneration of Amida Buddha and the hope for his western paradise fostered an iconography that derived from images of the court and from the tantric mandalas of Shingon Buddhism; and the gardens of the Jōdo sect, as it came to be called (from Saihō Jōdo, the Pure Land of the West), were conceived as mandalas symbolizing paradise. Because they were also the residences of the noblemen who commissioned them, these wealthy and powerful few were already dwelling – at least in principle – in the paradise to come. The gardens were inevitably extremely formal and symmetrical; their shapes and their structures were manifestations of courtly elegance. Temple buildings and residences alike perpetuated traditional court architecture, and the gardens made characteristic use of bodies of water to provide, from different viewpoints, the illusion of distance and the sense that objects, perspectives, and edifices were floating on their own reflections.

The use of water in the Jōdo gardens in turn had its origin in the Heian court gardens, the "dream gardens," of the ninth century, with their emphasis on artificial lakes and streams. And before the Heian lake gardens there were, of course, the formal lake gardens of China with their carefully composed views of water and islands, their bridges and standing rocks. In the mid–ninth century the nobility began to plan gardens that deliberately evoked the wilder landscapes of other parts of Japan. Peninsulas planted with trees reached out into lakes. Lakeshores were covered with pebbles to represent ocean beaches. The attempt to suggest living landscapes worked against the urge of symmetrical formality and helped to lighten it and render its symbolism subtler and more complex. By the eleventh century the principles of the Heian gardens – conceived then, of course, as the correct principles for all gardens – were established conventions that could be summarized in *Treatise on Garden Making* by Tachibana Toshitsuna, the son of an important political figure of the period. Toshitsuna set forth the rules for making ponds, lakes, and waterfalls, and for arranging and planting trees and growing things, all with a doctrinaire finality that includes his detailed predictions of the catastrophes awaiting heretics who might presume to do things in any other way. The rules of Heian gardening had become superstitions, and some of this development may have derived from elements of Chinese geomancy whose meanings, by To-shitsuna's period, were no longer clearly remembered.

We do not know what Musō had learned of the art of garden design by the time he undertook to design the garden of Saihō-ji, but he was surely acquainted with the main currents of these traditions and must have been familiar with many court and temple gardens. Saihō-ji combines aspects of the paradise gardens of the Jōdo sect with far fewer of the symmetrical inventions generally considered manifestations of the spirit of Zen. There is a lake with an island in it, and a wandering series of rocks. A path meanders along the winding lakeshore.

One of the conditions (one of the materials, indeed) of the art of gardening, whatever gardeners may think of it, is the role of change, which makes gardening particularly appropriate to Buddhism. Nothing stays as the hand of the gardener leaves it or as the mind of the gardener originally conceives of it, and although Musō in his gardens made extensive and original use of such things as rocks, which change so slowly that they can be taken as symbols of permanence, those gardens of his that later generations saw and see are inevitably different from those he would have seen in his lifetime. Trees and all living things there have grown, died, been replaced. Shadows and leaves fall differently even in those gardens that have been cared for and kept as close as possible to the way he designed them. Saihō-ji itself is famous, among other things, for something that has changed enormously since the time of Musō's original garden and, in the view of most commentators, could have had no place in his plan. The ground under the trees by the lake, and in other sections of the garden reached by stone steps, is covered with a profusion of different mosses that curl like waves around the arrangements of large stones on the upper levels. It is said that these celebrated mosses, or at least many of them, spread through parts of the garden only in the nineteenth century when the temple became too poor to be able to maintain the garden. Yet there may well have been some mosses in the original plan. For instance, up on the hillside there is a detail that recurs in a number of Musō's gardens, a dry waterfall in which large vertical stones suggest the cascading of water. And at the foot of the stone waterfall there is a basin brimming not with water but with moss.

In the same year that the garden at Saihō-ji was laid out, perhaps on the site of an earlier garden, Emperor Go-Daigo died. Musō urged the Ashikagas, Takauji and Tadayoshi, to build a temple dedicated to the spirit of the dead emperor whom they had deposed, a project that might help to restore harmony between the old dynasty and the new one. The site chosen had once been an imperial estate, with a Heian lake garden. Musō's plans transformed it into the present temple enclosure and garden of Tenryū-ji, a labor that took five years. Parts of the garden appear in some of Musō's poems – its dry waterfall; its lake, named Hui-neng's Pond after the Sixth Zen Patriarch; its West Mountains (Arashiyama). The garden combines a great sweep of landscape and a feeling of space with one of intimacy and simplicity. Along with Zuisen-ji in Kamakura, with its cave and ponds, and the pond garden at Kenchō-ji in Kamakura, it is considered one of the works that best exemplifies Musō's conception and style of garden design. Perhaps appropriate to the vision of emptiness that he himself taught in all his arts, his very role in its plan has been disputed, though there is a record of Ashikaga Takauji's directive to him to turn the old imperial estate into a temple compound.

Musō's work on gardens filled the last decade of his life. He managed to combine it with teaching and advisory and administrative duties. In his late years he settled in the small riverside temple of Rinsen-ji, on the Ōi River at the edge of Kyoto. Once an imperial villa, Rinsen-ji had been converted into a temple by Emperor Go-Daigo as a shrine for his second son, who had died there. The emperor had made Musō the temple's first abbot, as Musō was later to become the first abbot of Tenryū-ji, and at Rinsen-ji too Musō redesigned the garden. But at Rinsen-ji his work has completely disappeared, as a result of war and neglect. The present garden there, a stone and gravel enclosure in the style of the famous one at Ryōan-ji, across the city, is a modern addition.

It was at Rinsen-ji, on September 29, 1351, that Musō wrote a final poem:

> In the real world
>   the pure world
>   no separation exists
> why wait
>   for another time
>   and another meaning
> of the teaching
>   on Vulture Peak

is here today
who else
are you looking for
to preserve the Way

He died on the following day, September 30, at the age of seventy-seven. Cremation was not then the invariable rule for the disposal of bodies, and Musō was buried at the end of the main hall of worship. The slabs of rock covering his tomb, which can be seen from outside the building, lie under the floor of the shrine; a rock formation beside them resembles a chain of mountains in a Sung dynasty painting. Over the tomb, two fluorescent light tubes have been attached to the beams under the floor. Above, in the raised shrine, is a wooden statue of Musō that looks life-size. He is seated in what is no doubt zazen posture. The carved robes flow down from the raised seat to the floor. His hands are in the meditation mudra and his eyes are half-closed. One can see even in the likeness the gentleness that distinguished him as a child.

Musō had had some 13,145 recorded students: monks, nuns, and laity, including seven emperors. Fifty-two of his students received his approval as successors and a number of them in turn became renowned teachers. He had founded fourteen temples in Kyoto, Kamakura, and other parts of Japan. Upon his death his writings, collected by his followers, included three volumes of conversations, which became *Dialogues in the Dream*, a volume of sermons, and the volume of poems from which the present translation has been made.

The arts that Musō practiced – poetry, painting, calligraphy, garden design – depended, as all arts do, on a balance of convention and control, on the one hand, and spontaneity on the other. There is an inevitable tension between the two elements, and yet ideally the two seem to give life to each other and become one. The gardens with their varying evocations of what is considered natural are elaborately controlled manifestations of the conventions that Musō inherited and developed, though Musō is said to have favored a freer and less artificial style than was fashionable in his day.

His poetry was written both in Japanese and in Chinese, in two traditional forms, more than half of it in the gāthās – Chinese four-line verses – that had become conventional in the world of Zen in China before Zen passed to Japan. It was customary for students of Ch'an, as the teaching was called in China, to write a verse to express what they had understood, after they had had what they considered to be an experience of satori, or insight into the nature of reality. The custom was established by the time of the *Platform Sutra of the Sixth Patriarch* in the latter part of the eighth century. In that important Zen text a crucial turn of the story of the Sixth Patriarch depends upon two gāthās, the first composed by a monk at the Fifth Patriarch's monastery, which translates:

> The body is the Bodhi tree
> The mind is a clear mirror
> Always keep the mirror polished
> Let no dust gather on it

The other gāthā, attributed by legend to the Sixth Patriarch, survives in various forms. The most famous of them might be translated:

Bodhi has no tree
The mirror rests on nothing
From the beginning not a thing is
Where would the dust alight?

Later, during the Sung dynasty, when several of the famous teachers gathered the Zen teaching devices known as koans into books, the compilers, or later successors, appended gāthās to most of the koans to confirm and extend the thrust of the teaching they embodied. The practice continued into Musō's lifetime. Keizan Jōkin (1268–1325), a great teacher and a poet who lived earlier in the century during which Musō was born, composed a volume called the Denkō-roku, or Transmission of the Lamp, a purported compilation of the enlightenment experiences of each of the Patriarchs, from Shākyamuni Buddha to Keizan's own teacher, Dōgen. Each of the stories was followed, or "capped," by a poem, sometimes though not always a gāthā. And since Keizan was a gifted poet, some of the poems have a clear beauty that does not depend on context.

Musō wrote poems throughout the whole of his adult life, and some are Zen poems in this somewhat ritualized sense. The "Satori Poem" (110) is an example. Some are poems on the deaths of friends, and, like all Musō's poems, they too express their subject from the viewpoint of Zen experience. His poems

on the visits and departures of friends, which continue another
convention of Chinese poetry, are written in the Zen spirit, as
are his most obviously personal poems: the poems of reminis-
cence and those arising directly from circumstances in his own
life, such as the ones about his hut in Miura. These seem to
have within their ancestry the poems of the eighth-century
Chinese poet Wang Wei, himself a Ch'an (Zen) student during
the T'ang dynasty, the golden age of Ch'an.

Since gāthās have usually been translated into English as
quatrains, perhaps it is necessary to explain the form used to
translate Musō's gāthās in this collection. The explanation is
really my collaborator's, who supplied the first literal versions of
these poems in English, with the lines already broken into three
sections as they are here. When I asked him why, he wrote to
me, "We Japanese Zen priests are expected to learn the tradi-
tional chanting of Zen poetry. Even Musō, I think, must have
chanted his own poetry just as we do now." He gave several
examples, one from a poem of Musō's, the "Satori Poem":

多	年	掘	地	覓	青	天
ta	*nen*	*hotte*	*chi*	*motomu*	*sei*	*ten*
many	year	dig	ground	seek	blue	heaven

which he said would be chanted in Japanese:

Ta-ne-n-n-n
 chio-o-hot-te-e-e
  sei-i-ten-n-n-o-o-o-moto-o-o-mu-u-u-u-u

"In chanting," he said, "a pause matters much, I think... Truly no translator has ever broken lines. Even D.T. Suzuki didn't. It may be right so far as form is concerned. But I wish to hear Musō's chanting. Unless you feel some awkwardness as English poetry, I myself would like to keep all the poems as they are. If forced to make a choice, I dare to prefer his unheard voices to his written form."

I have since heard the chanting in Shigematsu-san's father's temple, but the broken line, in English, suggested something quite different to me, of course: the breathless rush of Maya-kovsky (as it comes across in translation) and above all the delicacy, lightness, and penetrating plainness of the later work of William Carlos Williams. Whatever the original appropriateness of the innovation, I was happy to keep it and to try to make it seem the right form for Musō's poems in English.

As might be guessed from the fact that the translation is a collaboration, I cannot read the original languages: neither the classical Chinese of Musō's poems nor the formal medieval Japanese of his prose. The translation was meant to be as faithful a representation of Musō in English as I could provide with the help of those who could read those languages, but it was not intended for scholars or for those who could read the original. There have been, until now, almost no translations of Musō into English. He is mentioned, of course, in D.T. Suzuki's histories of Zen, but I made my more extensive acquaintance with his work in the biographical and critical writing of Masumi Shibata, and in the French translations Shibata has made with his French wife Maryse. They have published (Editions G.P.

Maisonneuve and Larose, Paris, 1974) the whole of the *Muchū Mondō* in French, as *Dialogues dans le Rêve*. Soon after I had found that work, conversations with Sōiku Shigematsu led to him sending me, from Japan, the first literal versions of some of Musō's poems, and our collaboration began. We have worked on the versions sporadically over the course of several years, from the first exchanges of letters to a theoretically final set of marginal notes that we revised, sitting out the rain under the eaves of the abbot's quarters at Tenryū-ji, looking out at the garden that Musō had designed there, at Hui-neng's Pond, the West Mountains in the mist, the stone waterfall, the stone bridge.

As for the poems, I know only what I have been able to hear from – and, as it were, through – the literals. In such translations, as in all translation, one knows well enough what one was listening for in English, what one would like the translations to be: living poems in the new language, poems that manage to represent the life of the originals. It is too much to hope for, as we all know, and yet one goes on, out of the nature of necessity and of language, trying to put into words that life. Where is it? A poem of Keizan's in the *Denkō-roku* goes something like this:

The water is clear all the way down.
Nothing ever polished it. That is the way it is.

–W.S.M.
Peahi, Maui, 1989

Wandering

A runaway son
  will never come
    into his own
My treasure
  is the cloud on the peak
    the moon over the valley
Traveling east or west
  light and free
    on the one road
I don't know whether
  I'm on the way
    or at home

A Lodging House in Town

Right among the people coming and going
   I have a place to stay
     I shut the gate even in the daytime
and feel as though I had bought
   Wo-chou the great mountain
     and had it with me in town
Never since I was born
   have I liked to argue
     mouth full of blood
My mouth is made fast
   to heaven and earth
     so the universe is still

Buddha's Satori

For six years sitting alone
  still as a snake
    in a stalk of bamboo
with no family
  but the ice
    on the snow mountain
Last night
  seeing the empty sky
    fly into pieces
he shook
  the morning star awake
    and kept it in his eyes

For Taihei Oshō

I won't let even
   the Buddha and Patriarchs
      through my gate
so I never thought
   to welcome some guests
      and roll my eyes at others
I open the gate a little
   to thank you
      for your visit
and at once the mountains
   and the rivers stand up
      and start the famous dance

Reizan Oshō Visits Me

I leave to the highborn
all the honors
of this dissolving world
A life of poverty
has taught me to love
haze and mist
Today in the spring
the friendship between us
adds warmth to the sunlight
Even a dry post
here on the shore
is blossoming

6

I'm not so deep in it
    as that hermit who held up
      his fist to the guest
but deep enough
    Reizan Oshō
      for us to be able to talk
Beyond my garden
    the sea begins
      level and boundless
Don't echo Chao-chou's
    "the water's too shallow
      to anchor here"

Reply to Reizan Oshō

I don't go out
  to wander around
    I stay home here in Miura
while time flows
  on through
    the unbounded world
In the awakened eye
  mountains and rivers
    completely disappear
the eye of delusion
  looks out upon
    deep fog and clouds
Alone on my zazen mat
  I forget the days
    as they pass
The wisteria has grown
  thick over the eaves
    of my hut
The subtle Way
  of Bodhidharma –
    I never give it a thought
Does anyone know
  the truth of Zen
    or what to ask about it?

Thanks for Daisen Oshō's Visit

Here I have enough to eat
and I have taken root
far from the world
People who like to find fault
can melt even gold with their talk
why should I listen to that
My mind is weightless
and without color
like the lingering fog
The sound of the evening waves
wakes me
from my afternoon nap
Cradled in the breast of this mountain
I have forgotten
its original wildness
Day after day
watching the sea
I have never seen its depths
If I cannot attain
the very heart
of Zen
a wave a thousand miles long
will rise up and heave
on the sea beyond my gate

9

Chick feed is what I eat
    a quail's nest is where I live
        here by the sea
It's all so cramped and huddled
    the waves almost touch
        the fishermen's huts
It's certainly no place
    for entertaining
        the rich and famous
and yet a single bubble
    contains the whole
        limitless sky

Loud thunder
   rattles the mountains
      around this remote village
All at once
   my seclusion my quiet –
      where are they
Don't say that my mouth
   is too small to tell
      of the beauty of the world
In the corner of the garden
   in the winter the plum trees
      are announcing spring

Thanks Sent to Taihei Oshō

I have been lazy
   ever since I was born
      it would be hard to change now
so I've hidden
   my lump of a body
      near the edge of the sea
Today Taihei Oshō of Ungan-ji
   surprises me
      with a visit
I shake his hand
   and we smile
      in the one wind

From My Hut in Miura

Leaving my footprints
　　nowhere
　　　　south or north
I go into hiding
　　here by the bay full of moonlight
　　　and the misty hill
I love the life that remains to me
　　here out of sight in the water
　　　my scales dimmed
I have no wish to leap
　　up the Dragon Gate Falls
　　　to turn into a dragon

13

In these mountain villages and harbor towns
   I'm happy to have found
      good company
a crowd of fishermen
   in and out of my hut
      the whole time
Since I have never held out
   the least thing
      by way of bait
I've managed not to betray
   the fish who have approached
      at the risk of their lives

From the beginning
   the crooked tree
      was no good for a lordly dwelling
how could anyone
   expect the nobles
      to use it for their gates
Now it's been thrown out
   onto the shore
      of this harbor village
handy for the fishermen
   to sit on
      while they're fishing

East of the strait
  beside my hut
    I fish in silence
no more chatter about
  pure land
    impure land
Don't get the idea
  that I'm hoarding salt
    from the black market
I can't cheat the public
  like the one
    who dozed on the bridge

My thatched hut
   the whole sky
      is its roof
the mountains are its hedge
   and it has the sea
      for a garden
I'm inside
   with nothing at all
      not even a bag
and yet there are visitors
   who say "It's hidden
      behind a bamboo door"

All on my own I'm happy
  in the unmapped landscape
    inside the bottle
my only friend
  is this
    wisteria cane
Last night
  we stayed up talking
    so late
that I'm afraid
  I was overheard
    by the empty sky

Heaven Peak

Blue blue the summit
    soars above
        fog and cloud
steep and rough
    it stands against
        the empty sky
Everyone who looks up
    gazes in awe
        it seems to go on forever
and each one sees
    the mountains of the earth
        holding it up

Gem Mountain

It towers
   from the beginning
      without a flaw
The rain beats upon it
   the wind cuts it
      it only shines brighter
Even fog and cloud
   cannot hide the path
      to the summit
Lin Hsiang-ru was wrong
   running his errand
      to the Ch'in castle

Another Summit

It soars alone
   its power stands apart
      from the other mountains
Those who see it
   feel their eyes
      widen
Ever since the boy Sudhana
   was bewildered
      by Meghashri
the blue haze
   the red mist
      have not come to rest

Bamboo Garden

The third one crooked the second one leaning
    bamboos have grown
        by the stone steps of the garden
every year
    there are more of them
        until now they are a forest
At the clack of a stone on a bamboo
    Hsiang-yen shattered
        the uncountable worlds
but this garden
    continues in its green shade
        just as before

To the Emperor's Messenger

The affairs of the world
    are nothing to me
        I am tired of coming and going
this poor hut is perfect for me
    the one possession
        of a monk who does nothing
In the stove
    there is no fire
        and no potato
so I have no time
    to wipe my mouth
        to greet the emperor's messenger

Old Creek

Since before anyone remembers
    it has been clear
        shining like silver
though the moonlight penetrates it
    and the wind ruffles it
        no trace of either remains
Today I would not dare
    to expound the secret
        of the streambed
but I can tell you
    that the blue dragon
        is coiled there

Snow Valley

Each drifting snowflake
   falls nowhere
      but here and now
Under the settling flowers of ice
   the water is flowing
      bright and clear
The cold stream
   splashes out
      the Buddha's words
startling
   the stone tortoise
      from its sleep

Dry Tree

Leaning all by himself
 on the icy rock
  he has lost all his warmth
His skins have peeled away
 but still he has not seen
  the wonderland
Now flowers
 have opened
  outside of heaven and earth
and spring winds are blowing there
 nobody knows
  where they are

Old Man in Retirement

I stop worrying about anything
   I give up activities
      I'm full of my life
I no longer
   go to the temple
      evening and morning
If they ask me
   "What are you doing
      in your old age"
I smile and tell them
   "I'm letting my white hair
      fall free"

Strange Peak

Looming up
   rough and steep
      what force
The trees look like works of magic
   and all of the stones
      are possessed of powers
Once you climb the peak
   your eyes
      will start from your head
but until then
   it stands veiled in unbroken
      fog and mist

Poem on Dry Mountain (A Zen Garden)

A high mountain
   soars without
      a grain of dust
a waterfall
   plunges without
      a drop of water
Once or twice
   on an evening of moonlight
      in the wind
this man here
   has been happy
      playing the game that suited him

At the Nachi Kannon Hall

The Milky Way
    pours waterfalls
        over this human world
the cold
    rushing tumbling sounds
        echo through the blue sky
Veneration
    to the Great Compassionate
        Avalokiteshvara
How lucky I am
    to have no trouble
        hearing

Spring Cliff

Everywhere
   soft breeze warm sunshine
      the same calm
Even the withered trees
   on the dark cliff
      are blossoming
I tried to find
   where Subhūti
      meditates
but suddenly in the shadow
   of mist and fog
      the path splits a thousand ways

Reply to Gen'nō Oshō's Poem

You climb
    Mount Hiei
        on ladders of cloud
I walk
    out of Kyoto
        with a wisteria cane
A thousand miles apart
    like the stars of the east
        and the stars of the north
and this is our one chance
    to remind each other
        that we are friends

For the Death of a Monk

They say that an accident
  is like
    a bellows
but isn't it better
  to go directly
    to the town of Nirvana
Now a spring wind
  is playing for you the tune
    "Return to the Origin"
and even the Buddha's hands
  cannot interfere
    with your homecoming

33

People's abuse
   has melted what was golden
      and it has gone from the world
Fortune and misfortune
   both belong to the land
      of dreams
Don't look back
   to this world
      your old hole in the cellar
From the beginning
   the flying birds have left
      no footprints on the blue sky

To Kengai Oshō of Engaku-ji

Old Man Ho
    once paid the master of the hut
      a surprise visit
Nowhere in the universe
    is it possible to hide
      one's idle everyday life
Yesterday you came
    from Deer's Joy Mountain
      all the way to my hut
and as it happened
    I was not even
      on this mountain

Moon Mountain

The light of awakening
　appears when it has been
　　forgotten
High and vast the mountain
　lifts forth
　　the moon
I myself
　have climbed to
　　the summit
In the world outside of things
　there is nothing
　　to get in the way

Free Old Man

His original way
  is plain and simple
    not caught up in things
He preaches the dharma
  at liquor stores
    and fish shops
He pays no attention
  to sacred rituals
    or secular conventions
Thick white eyebrows
  in his old age
    signs of enlightenment

37

Visiting My Old Hut in Late Spring

At one time I lived
　for several years
　　on this beach
now I come
　wandering along here
　　as a visitor
The trees around the hut
　still remember me
　　and the green
that returns after the flowers
　offers me once more
　　what is left of the spring

38

On the blue waves
   the sun glitters
      the mist is burned away
then the mountains appear
   soaring close to the shore
      each one the most beautiful
Already I have loaded the boat
   to the sinking point
      with the joy of the passing spring
Even Confucius
   who smiled at his disciple's laughter
      would envy what I see

39

Laughing Mountain

Originally it does not need
  to have Ma-tsu step
    on its foot
Ageless cliff with brushwood grown
  never changing
    from the beginning
It doesn't look high or rugged
  at first nobody sees
    how dangerous it is
But the cloud and mist around it
  hide a forest
    of swords

Inauguration of Fukusan Dormitory

Sacred and secular
  originally live
    in the same house
With compassionate hands
  the Great Master has opened
    the gate for the first time
Don't ask who
  or how many
    are in the hall
These tiles and rafters
  contain all
    of heaven and earth

Cloud Mountain

Living secluded
    above the cloud
        at the top of Mount Sū
abiding in your origin
    you demonstrate
        the truth of Zen
The sharp sword of wisdom
    raised between your eyebrows
        rests in your palms
You have moved far from town
    from now on you renew
        the Way of Bodhidharma

At Gen's Embarkation for Yuan China

Deep grief wringing the heart
   promising over and over to meet again
     you leave Deer's Joy Mountain
The colors of spring
   in a hundred castle gardens
     all live in your staff
Now that you have known
   the great death
     once and for all
may the original sail
   bring you east
     again to this land

43

At Kan's Embarkation for Yuan China

Setting out over the sea to the south
   looking for the truth
     but it's too late
Sailing all that way
   what do you hope to find
     over the ocean
Right here and now
   I'll spare you thirty blows
     for a while
and wait for you to come back
   some day
     in brocade robes

44

At Iku's Embarkation for Yuan China

Whale billows
   thousands of miles
      all the way to the end of the sky
don't betray
   the boundless clear wind
      and the bright moon
When you have
   worn out
      your straw sandals
you will be back
   leaping free
      of the pit of Nang-yang

Mourning for the Layman
Named Cloud Peak

In your old age
    giving up your career you lived
        free of the concerns of the world
you gave no more thought
    to your own achievements
        that had cost you such sweat
In the hollow night
    the ship sails on
        but where is it going
Age after age
    you will raise a green peak
        through the clouds

Patriarch Peaks

Twenty-eight Indian Patriarchs
   six Chinese all reveal
      the subtle working of Zen
Higher and higher
   they soar into the blue sky
      dwarfing the five summits of Mount Sumeru
Naturally their successors
   come and try
      to climb their peaks
The dharma that has reached
   its golden summit
      never falls away

47

East Peak

From the beginning
    people have gazed in awe at Taigaku
      the East Peak
It shoots up into the heavens
    on it the sun rises
      the moon rises
Its original blue and yellow
    are not among the colors
      of other mountains
It will hold the spring sunlight
    year after year
      after year

Old Hut

A handful of thatch
   has sheltered its master's head
     since before time began
Now some new students
   are gathering to wait
     outside the gate
Don't say
   there's nothing
     new at all
Year after year
   in this garden
     the trees blossom

Tengan Oshō's Visit to Erin-ji

With your tall
  golden staff tinkling
    you have come all the way down
Talking for days
  about things not of the world
    our words have been all we needed
Sumptuous the colors
  of the halls
    and the temple buildings
Lush and dense around them
  the serene beauty of the forest
    and the arbored walks
Lovely! Our hearts are open
  Not a grain of sand
    in our friendship
May it go on just like this!
  In the floating world of things
    needles hide in the carpet
The memory of this visit
  should be handed down
    forever
There is something beyond happiness
  inside the gate
    of this mountain

Living in the Mountains:
Ten Poems

50

In this small hut
  are worlds beyond number
Living here alone
  I have endless company
Already I have
  attained the essence
How could I dare
  to want something higher

Among rocks and valleys
    deep in the folds of this mountain
the dharma does not go
    up or down
Having seen through
    old Huang-lung's mind
I plant vegetables
    around my meditation seat

Very high this mountain
   and few find their way up here
Only puffs of cloud
   drift up and past
As I meditate my original self
   empties all of heaven and earth
not at all like the lantern
   in broad day

All worries and troubles
    have gone from my breast
and I play joyfully
    far from the world
For a person of Zen
    no limits exist
The blue sky must feel
    ashamed to be so small

54

A curtain of cloud hangs
    before the meditation seat
an ice wheel of moonlight
    turns through the railing
Don't say I have erased
    all trace of attainment
Behind me there are still
    heaven and earth

Don't ask suspiciously
    why I have shut the gate
       and remain alone
Hiding light
   is the way
     one gives light
Thunder roars and roars
    until nobody
      hears it
On the other hand people say
    that the valley is so deep
      the dragon comes out late

56

I wake from my noon nap
   and see the shadows
      moving in the afternoon
Mist fades from the old cedar
   and I am face to face
      with Haku Mountain
Thirty years
   so many events
      have come and gone
Now I let them all go
   and sit in the stillness
      and am still

57

Green mountains
  have turned yellow
    so many times
the troubles and worries
  of the world of things
    no longer bother me
One grain of dust in the eye
  will render the Three Worlds
    too small to see
When the mind is still
  the floor where I sit
    is endless space

58

Time for a walk
   in the world outside
      and a look at who I am
Originally I had no cares
   and I am seeking
      nothing special
Even for my guests
   I have nothing
      to offer
Except these white stones
   and this clear
      springwater

With compassionate hands
   Buddha and Patriarchs
      constantly save those who are lost
Crimes and errors
   fill the whole sky
      and who knows it
Is there anything better
   than to stay at the foot
      of this misty cliff
watching in meditation
   the calm clouds
      on their way home to the cave

◆ ◆ ◆

Pine Shade

A hedge
   of a thousand trees
      standing in the cold
The green haze
   so deep and dense
      it keeps out the light
Don't blame me
   for staying alone
      with my door shut
The guidepost
   always stood open
      for anyone who passed

Plum Window

The flowers on one tree have opened
   and six houses
      are full of the sweet scent
I have managed to transmit
   the Sixth Patriarch's
      fragrant teaching
Now all the counties
   are made happy
      by the coming of spring
What monkey
   still hangs back
      in dreamland

Jewel Field

I have cultivated
 a piece of overgrown
  wasteland
All the soil now
 is beginning
  to shed light
Autumn
 is the time
  of harvest
Each grain gathered
 is worth
  several castles

Truth Hall

First the outer gate
   then the inner gate
      under the high roof the low roof
Deep within
   there is no argument
      to be heard
Each of you be sure
   to find the deepest truth
      in yourself
and say "Maitreya
   Buddha of the future
      no more, thank you!"

No Precedent

Beyond any
    link with the world
        he really is
To him the Buddha's and Patriarchs'
    preachings are
        wasted breath
He has gone now
    leaving behind nothing
        nothing at all
The great roc
    will never rest
        in the green paulownia branches

Old Man To-The-Point

No inheritance
   is like that from a true
      heir of the dharma
and there is no other school
   or different sect
      with which to quarrel
In your old age
   you have gone deeper
      into the truth under everything
and your eyebrows
   have grown down
      over your chin

Old Man Advancing

Beyond the point where the rivers
    end and the mountains vanish
       you have kept on walking
Originally
    the treasure lies
       just under one's feet
You made the mistake of thinking
    that now you would be able
       to retire in peace
Look: in your own hut
    the meditation mat
       has never been warm

Abiding Mountain

A violent storm
   beats against it
      but it never moves at all
Wild and solitary
   sharp and full of power
      it soars like a bird's feather
I give my assent only
   to one who has climbed
      to the summit
Walking sitting lying down
   he does everything as though
      he were out for a stroll

Snow Garden

Flowers with six petals
   have covered the whole ground
     and frozen everywhere
Heaven and earth have disappeared
   into this one
     pure color
A pine and a cedar
   by the stone stairs
     are still green
Shen-kuan
   must have lost sight of the mind
     of the great vessel

One Hut

The endless worlds
 have all gathered
  in this small hut
In the four directions
 and above and below
  there is no neighbor
All living beings
 secular and sacred
  live in here
Old Man Ho
 why do you go off visiting
  somebody else

Moon Tree Cliff

The moon trees keep growing and growing
    their blossoms sweep
        the wide ribbon of cloud
No one
    has ever climbed the high branches
        hidden in leaves
Subhūti has sat in his cave
    for years on end
        with his mind far away
not knowing that he is
    in the moon tree cave
        on the moon

Gem Creek

The mysterious valley fountain
  is originally bright and clear
    it was not made by humans
The banks on both sides
  and the stream between them
    all shine with one light
Without ruffling the surface
  look carefully
    into the depths
You'll see the uncountable
  legendary jewels
    of the Kunlun Mountains

No-Word Hut

I left my locked mouth
   hanging
      on the wall
With the brushwood
   door shut tight
      I delight in my own freedom
Inside
   my secret talk resounds
      like thunder
Even the bare
   posts and the lamps
      can't pretend they don't hear it

Old Mountain

Out of the green of spring
   and the yellow of autumn
      all by yourself you went
into the numberless mountains
   and you have stayed there
      hidden for many years
Even the clouds
   shun those peaks
      nothing obstructs the view
The eternal landscape
   of no season
      is spread before you

No End Point

The whole world is clear and empty
   to the ten directions
      There is no end point
And yet when we
   look carefully
      there is one after all
You fly out of this world
   looking backward
      riding the giant roc
into the hollow of a lotus thread
   to live there where heaven and earth
      were never divided

Lover of Mountains

Your compassionate mind
    soars like a summit
        there is your true effortless nature
some places smooth and gentle
    some places rugged and
        unapproachable
The mountain has
    no wish to be
        looked up to
It is only people
    who look up
        in wonder

76

Sūzan Oshō's Visit

Mountains on all sides
   rivers looped around it
      there's no trail to my hut
When the dragon-elephant approaches
   a path opens
      all by itself
In the hour of soaring talk
   neither has to think
      of meeting the other halfway
though all of you
   keep wandering into
      yes and no

Reply to Sūzan Oshō's Snow Poem

In one night
   ice flowers have filled
      all the forests and rivers
There shining clearly
   is Bodhidharma's guidepost
      a thousand years old
Inside the one color
   there is no
      stir of Zen
Shen-kuan stands in vain
   in snow
      up to his waist

The Pure Sound Pavilion of the Riverside Temple

The monastery
   like the moon in the water –
      heaven and earth are wide
The pavilion is reflected
   a hundred pavilions
      a thousand
A complete existence
   nothing missing nothing left over
      no need for the water to wash the ears clear
Day and night
   outside the gate
      the wide river flows

For Gen the New Head Priest of Erin-ji

Not leaving your
 Zen practice behind
  in the dreams of the Heavenly Palace
all by yourself
 you realize the elegance
  beyond elegance
Your old staff tinkling
 in the chilling dew and frost
  pierces heaven
In the Temple of the Forest of Wisdom
 the fruit is ripe
  now is the time

For Myō's Departure for Anzen-ji

Now the splendor of the Patriarch's Garden
    is smudged with the rising
        dust of war
Everywhere
    Zen students are sitting
        on mats of needles
No doubt your visit
    will bring good fortune
        upon the Temple of the Joy of Zen
The chill wind of wisdom
    from one tinkling staff
        is worth worlds beyond number

For Myō's Departure for Shōfuku-ji

A single true man
   appears in the world
     and all falsehood vanishes
No need to worry
   that the Way of the Patriarchs
     seems to be declining
This time
   your ax of wisdom
     has found wings
Someday
   surely it will rise up
     and fly

For Tetsu the New Head Priest of Erin-ji

For a long time
　　the world
　　　　has been decaying
The Way of the Patriarchs
　　declines day by day
　　　　nothing to do about it
Good! Now the one monk
　　whose hands are never
　　　　tucked in his sleeves
enters
　　the Forest of Wisdom
　　　　with his ax held high

For Shō the New Head Priest of Erin-ji

Actions to save the world
   have their ups and downs
      depending on circumstances
You have to be as careful
   as though you were dragging half a ton
      by a hair
Spare no efforts
   to bring the dharma rain
      to this countryside
The Forest of Wisdom
   will grow dense
      and cover the world

At Whole-World-In-View Hut

The heavens allowed me
    to settle myself
        on a small piece of land
Looking into the distance
    digging far down
        I delight in my own freedom
All who come here
    feel the lids fall
        from their eyes
This view
    of the world without end –
        there is nowhere to hide

Ashikaga Tadayoshi's Palace

When the blind is raised
    at the clear window
        one is facing the East Mountains
The magnificent landscape
    stretches away
        from the edge of the table
Everyone feels the silk veil
    drawn back
        from before his face
Illusions carried
    through many lives
        vanish in one moment

Climbing Down the Snowy Mountain

From inside the room
  you can't tell whether it's snowing
    outside or not
Don't judge
  Zen students
    sorting them into three piles
Sometimes one of them
  will bolt suddenly
    out to the endless mountains
kick over a peak
  and grind it
    underfoot

Snow at Rōhatsu Sesshin

I have slept by the cold window
  and come back
    from the land of dreams
The eye of my mind
  has opened by itself
    with no need of the morning star
All of heaven and earth
  hold up this mountain
    covered with snow
Where in the world
  is there a place
    for Shākyamuni to practice

It

One by one many leaves
   the colors of autumn
      let go of their twigs and fall
The cold cloud full of rain
   passes above
      the hollow of the mountain
Everyone alive
   is born gifted
      with true sight
How do you see
   these koans
      with your own eyes

Magnificent Peak

By its own nature
   it towers above
      the tangle of rivers
Don't say
   it's a lot of dirt
      piled high
Without end the mist of dawn
   the evening cloud
      draw their shadows across it
From the four directions
   you can look up and see it
      green and steep and wild

Reply to Bukkō Zenji's Poem at Seiken-ji

I remember that once
   my dharma grandfather
      was happy to visit here
I feel ashamed sometimes
   to be inferior still
      to the seagull he saw then
But I'm lucky
   to hold in one phrase
      all the words of all the ages
Above the sea
   the full moon
      is shining on the shore

Snow

Flowers of ice
   hide the heavens
      no more blue sky
a silver dust
   buries all the fields
      and sinks the green mountains
Once the sun
   comes out on the one
      mountaintop
even the cold
   that pierces to the bone
      is a joy

Gem Forest

Long shadows
   woven with light
      dispel all trees but these
Even the bead trees of Japan
   even gardenias
      are not worth admitting
Polished by wind
   buffed by rain
      a forest without a flaw
each leaf
   each branch
      a treasure alone of its kind

Withered Zen

Both sacred wisdom
 and ordinary feeling
  have completely fallen away
no craving
 for success and fame
  rises in my mind
Don't tell me that I've fallen
 into the cave
  on Stone Frost Mountain
Inside my heart
 I keep three thousand
  prancing chestnut horses

The Fragrance of the Udumbara

Once in a thousand years
    the Udumbara blooms
        It has opened its auspicious flowers
Many labored
    to bring it
        from India to Japan
Its heady fragrance
    lingers
        without fading
and is not lost
    among the thousand grasses
        the countless weeds

House of Spring

Hundreds of open flowers
  all come from
    the one branch
Look
  all their colors
    appear in my garden
I open the clattering gate
  and in the wind
    I see
the spring sunlight
  already it has reached
    worlds without number

No Gain

Virtue and compassion
    together make up
        each one's integrity
Nothing that comes through the gate
    from outside
        can be the family treasure
Throwing away
    the whole pile
        in your heart
with empty hands
    you come
        bringing salvation

By the Sea

Stretching into the distance
 the sea
  swallows a hundred rivers
for thousands of miles
 the spray joins the waves
  to the sky
What is true
 of the time you put up
  the old sail
Right there
 you come to know
  where it is

For Ko Who Has Come Back from China

A brief meeting today
    but it seems to gather up
        a hundred years
We have exchanged
    the compliments of the season
        that's word-of-mouth Zen
Don't say that
    your wisdom and my ignorance
        belong to opposing worlds
Look: China and Japan
    but there are not
        two skies

Ten Scenes in the
Dragon of Heaven Temple

The Gate of Universal Light

The great light of compassion
   illuminates this world
      in every part
As a boy
   Sudhana stood
      before the gates
When your eyelids
   have fallen across
      the whole of the empty world
the gate will open
   at the snap of a finger
      as it did then to let him pass

Incomparable-Verse Valley

The sounds of the stream
    splash out
        the Buddha's sermon
Don't say
    that the deepest meaning
        comes only from one's mouth
Day and night
    eighty thousand poems
        arise one after the other
and in fact
    not a single word
        has ever been spoken

Hall of the Guardian God

Inside the temple enclosure
   a place was set aside
      for a Shinto shrine
Wish with your whole self
   for the divine wind
      to help the Way of the Patriarchs
Don't ask why the pine trees
   in the front garden
      are gnarled and crooked
The straightness
   they were born with
      is right there inside them

Hui-neng's Pond

The dharma spring of the Sixth Patriarch
  has never run dry
    it is flowing even now
a single drop
  has fallen and spread
    far and deep
Don't be caught
  by the decorations at the edge
    and the wall around it
In the dead of night
  the moonlight strikes
    the middle of the pond

The Peak of the Held-Up Flower

On Vulture Peak
   once the Buddha
      held up a flower
It has been multiplied
   into a thousand plants
      one of them is on this mountain
Look: the fragrant seedlings
   have been handed all the way down
      to the present
No one knows
   how many spring winds are blowing
      in the timeless world

The Bridge Where the Moon Crosses

It arches like a rainbow
   dividing the stream
     joining the shores
one line
   a road bringing life
     crosses the quiet waves
It has carried
   donkeys across horses across
     but there is more to come
In the middle of the night
   the moon is crossing it
     pushing a cart

Three-Step Waterfall

At dangerous places
  awesome ledges
    three barriers
The loud water rushes
  The spray of the fall hovers
    It's hard to find the way
So many fish
  have fallen back
    with the stamp of failure on their foreheads
Who knows that this
  wind of blood
    is lashing the whole universe

Cave of the Thousand Pines

One heaven and earth
    deep in
        ten thousand pines
Green haze
    flickering
        hides the mouth of the cave
The heaven of a hermit
    belongs originally
        to a hermit
Don't say
    this place is not
        the earthly heaven

Dragon-Gate House

With no help
    from the Giant Spirit's
        mountain-shattering fist
the two peaks allowed
    a wide river
        to flow between them
Late at night
    no one
        is coming
Beyond the railing
    of the hut
        a few puffs of passing cloud

Turtle Head Stūpa

A pine tree
   with long needles
      has grown behind it
On top of the tower
   there is a Buddha image
      of eternal happiness
Now the doors and windows
   are all open
      and nothing inside is hidden
Dharma worlds
   beyond number
      are there for you to see

Tiger Valley

Steep mountains
    deep valley
        no one finds the way there
Tigers gather
    and fight
        fiercely together
The three saints
    crossing the bridge
        hand in hand
have mistaken the sound
    of the water
        for laughter

Tōki-no-Ge (Satori Poem)

Year after year
   I dug in the earth
      looking for the blue of heaven
only to feel
   the pile of dirt
     choking me
until once in the dead of night
   I tripped on a broken brick
     and kicked it into the air
and saw that without a thought
   I had smashed the bones
    of the empty sky

III

The Garden at the General's Residence

The beautiful landscape
   of the three famous god-mountains
      has all been reproduced here
Rough standing stones
   a stream meandering
      delight without end
How lovely! The setting
   for elegant play
      and serene pleasure
No doubt the dharma stream
   from the Sixth Patriarch's valley
      runs through here

Temple of Eternal Light

The mountain range
   the stones in the water
      all are strange and rare
The beautiful landscape
   as we know
      belongs to those who are like it
The upper worlds
   the lower worlds
      originally are one thing
There is not a bit of dust
   there is only this still and full
      perfect enlightenment

Mugoku Oshō's Snow Poem

Everyone sees
  only the falling
    scentless flowers
No one has yet understood
  where the flakes fly
    and where they fall
Now you excellent monk
  are sitting
    in the meditation hall
You know that the mind
  rises from the origin
    in the eighth consciousness, doesn't it

Sūzan Oshō's Visit to
My West Mountain Hut

A few puffs of white cloud
   drift around the mouth
      of the cave
without hindering
   my dharma friend when he comes
      to knock at my door
I've never found a way
   to hide my doing nothing
      day after day
We join hands
   and walk back and forth
      back and forth

On the Wall of Cloud-Friend Hut

The cliff
    towers beside the cave
        shutting out the light
Half the space
    in the six-foot bamboo hut
        is given over to cloud
Living alone
    a person takes
        pleasure in such things
not regretting
    the absence
        of swarming visitors

Digging Out the Buddha Relic

From under the ground
   it emerges into the world
      offering enlightenment
The small circle of light
   spreading around it
      holds the numberless worlds
It is hard
   to measure and weigh
      its rarity
Clear and light unmistakably
   there it lies
      by the hoe

Reply to a Friend's Poem

Our karma led
  you and me
    to live on separate mountains
It is hard to speak
  as the wind does
    across a thousand miles
But nothing comes between
  the cloud in Ch'u
    and the water in Yueh
Meeting in our old age
  we are happy to talk
    day and night

118

Ox Turned Loose

Ignoring lash and rope
   he moves along following
     the Original Nature
He is playing outside the fence
   he won't look back
     at anyone
There is no way
   that I could have found
     his tracks anywhere
but look he shows his whole body
   in worlds
     countless as dust and sand

Clear Valley

The water that can't be muddied
  with any stick
    is deeper than depth
The sky and the water
  are a single
    deepening blue
If you really want to find
  the source of the Sixth Patriarch's
    fountain
don't look for it
  on the one bank or on the other
    or in the middle of the stream

Old Man at Leisure

Sacred or secular
    manners and conventions
        make no difference to him
Completely free
    leaving it all to heaven
        he seems like a simpleton
No one catches
    a glimpse inside
        his mind
this old man
    all by himself
        between heaven and earth

Ancient Origin

One drop of dharma water
    from the Sixth Patriarch's valley
        was there before the first legendary Buddha
It comes from a great distance
    and I know that its source
        is far within
Pity the one who has not yet
    come home
        from over the sea
and goes on looking somewhere else
    for the great subtle mind
        of the Buddha of India

Old Man of Few Words

The silent old man
   asked me to write
      a poem for him
The silly contradictions
   in the one I composed
      made people laugh to death
Look carefully again
   at the truth
      of nonduality
then even Vimalakīrti's
   jaw will drop
      like bark from a birch tree

Jewel Cliff

Sharp facets
   a brightness
      not made by cutting
Eight faces
   clear and bright
      no stain anywhere
Good! Here is
   the very form
      of transcendent wisdom
Day and night
   all the gods in heaven
      will rain flowers upon it

Joy Mountain

Grasses and trees
  look different
    and the auspices are good
Puffs of cloud
  delight in trailing
    around the peak
A thousand mountains
  a million hills
    look up to its virtue
Is there anyone
  who has never been blessed
    with its shelter

For a Monk Going West

For many years
   our friendship
      has ripened
One morning
   you say good-bye
      and start down to the west
Stop trying to find the secret
   of succeeding
      as head priest
Look the sharp ax
   has been in your hands
      since the beginning

Flat Mountain

Broad and flat
   it emerges
      beyond height
Seven shoulders
   eight hollows
      all shelve to one plane
No one
   knows where
      the summit is
From the beginning
   there was never
      a path to it

Beyond the World

This place of wild land
  has no boundaries
    north south east or west
It is hard to see
  even the tree
    in the middle of it
Turning your head
  you can look beyond
    each direction
For the first time
  you know that your eyes
    have been deceiving you

Beyond Light

The clear mirror
   and its stand
      have been broken
There is no dust
   in the eyes
      of the blind donkey
Dark
   dark everywhere
      the appearance of subtle Zen
Let it be
   The garden lantern
      opens its mouth laughing

Hut in Harmony

When the master
   without a word
      raises his eyebrows
the posts and rafters
   the cross beams and rooftree
      begin to smile
There is another place
   for conversing
      heart to heart
The full moon
   and the breeze
      at the half-open window

Lamenting the Civil War

So many times since antiquity
   the human world
      has barely escaped destruction
yet ten thousand fortunes
   and a thousand misfortunes
      end in one void after all
Puppets squabbling
   back and forth
      across the stage
People brawling
   over a snail's horn
      winning or losing
The ferocity
   of a snipe and a clam
      glaring at each other
only to arrive after death
   before the tribunal
      of Yama the Judge of Hell
When will the horses of war
   be turned loose
      on Flower Mountain
It would be best
   to throw their bits away
      to the east of the Buddha's Palace

Notes to Musō's Poems (by poem number)

4   Taihei (in Japanese), literally "perfect peace."

6   Chao-chou once visited a hermit and said, "Hi, there." The latter held up his fist as his answer to the former. Then Chao-chou left the hut, saying, "The water's too shallow to anchor here." He then went to see another hermit, who also held up his fist. But this time Chao-chou nodded with affirmation. "Well, what's the difference?" This is a koan.

12   The Dragon Gate Falls: the famous Yu-Gate Falls in China. A legend relates the story of a carp that succeeds in climbing them and then turns into a dragon. Symbolically, the gateway represents success in one's career.

15   It is said that once Tan-hsia slept lying on the bridge leading to Lo-yang, to the surprise of the city official who discovered him.

17   In an old Chinese story, a man goes into the bottle with its owner, an old druggist on the street, and enjoys the land of wizards. (In Zen, this strange experience suggests that of satori.)

19   Lin was sent to the king of Ch'in, a neighboring country, because the latter proposed to exchange the noted flawless jewel owned by Lin's lord with the fifteen castles of Ch'in. But when Lin handed the jewel to the king, the latter broke his promise, pretending that he had forgotten

his offer. Lin asked the king to return the jewel to him so that he could reveal its one hidden flaw. Actually the jewel had no flaw. Thus Lin kept the jewel from falling into the enemy's hands and narrowly escaped with his life back to his country.

20 Sudhana visits fifty-three saints, seeking instruction. He wants to visit Meghashri, the very first teacher of the Buddhist truth, but looks for him in vain; seven days later he sees Meghashri walking on Another Summit. This is a koan.

22 The emperor is Go-Daigo.

25 "Dry Tree," *koboku* in Japanese: Koboku Jōei.

26 "Old Man in Retirement," *kyūō* in Japanese: Kyūō Fukan.

27 "Strange Peak," *kihō* in Japanese: Kihō Shiyū.

29 Nachi is noted for its falls; Kannon is the Japanese rendering of Avalokiteshvara, a bodhisattva of mercy, whose wish is to save the whole world.

34 Old Man Ho: Chao-chou. Cf. note 6. Engaku-ji is called "Zui-roku-san" – literally, a mountain full of deer, which suggests a good omen.

35 "Moon Mountain," *gassan* in Japanese: Gassan Shūsū

38 In *Lun-yü*, Confucius agreed with his disciple's words of joy in the passing spring.

39 "Laughing Mountain," *shōzan* in Japanese: Shōzan Shū-nen. Ma-tsu once kicked the chest of his disciple to lead him into satori.

40 Fukusan dormitory, the student hall built in Kenchō-ji in 1327. The "Great Master" suggests Seisetsu Shōchō and also Shākyamuni.

41 "Cloud Mountain," *unzan* in Japanese: Unzan Chietsu.

42 The "great death" is the complete death of one's own ego; from this once-and-for-all experience of emptiness starts a new Zen life.

44 Nang-yang once summoned his attendant monk three times, and the latter responded each time. The meaning of these three summonses and responses is a koan.

46 "Patriarch Peaks," *sohō* in Japanese: Sohō Pō.

47 "East Peak": layman Sagami Umenokami's dharma name.

48 "Old Hut," *koan* in Japanese: Kōan Fushō.

51 Huang-lung guided his students by the famous koan, "Huang-lung's Three Barriers."

57 The Three Worlds: the world of desire, of the five senses; the world of form but of no desire; the world of neither form nor desire.

60 Lin-chi planted pine trees as a guidepost for the younger generation.

63 "Truth Hall," or the first truth gate; *gidō* in Japanese: Gidō Shūshin.

64 "No Precedent," *muhan* in Japanese: Emperor Kōgon's dharma name after retirement.

65 Long eyebrows: symbol of a great man of satori.

69 Old Man Ho: Chao-Chou. Cf. note 6.

70 "Moon Tree Cliff," *keigan* in Japanese: Hosokawa Yoriyuki's dharma name.

71 "Gem Creek," *gyokuen* in Japanese: Hosokawa Yoriyuki's wife's dharma name.

72 "No-Word Hut," *mokuan* in Japanese: Mokuan Shūyu.

73 "Old Mountain," *kosan* in Japanese: Ashikaga Tadayoshi's dharma name.

74 "No End Point," *mugoku* in Japanese: Mugoku Shigen.

75 "Lover of Mountains," *ninzan* in Japanese: General Ashigaka Takauji's dharma name.

77 Sūzan (Mount Ch'ung) refers to the mountain where Bodhidharma lived. Shen-kuan stood buried in snow up to his waist, asking Bodhidharma's permission to be his disciple.

78 Pure Sound Pavilion: Bon'non-kaku. Riverside Temple: Rinsen-ji.

79 Erin-ji: literally, "Forest of Wisdom Temple."

80 Anzen-ji: literally, "Joy of Zen Temple."

81 Shōfuku-ji: literally, "Sacred Fortune Temple."

87 Rōhatsu, or December 8, is the day when Shākyamuni attained satori at the moment he saw the morning star. In celebration of it, each monastery holds a special intensive practice from December 1 to the morning of December 8.

90 Bukkō: literally, "Buddha's Light."

94 "The Fragrance of the Udumbara," *dompō* in Japanese: Dompō Shūō.

95 "House of Spring," *shun'oku* in Japanese: Shun'oku Myōha.

99 Dragon of Heaven Temple: Tenryū-ji. "The Gate of Universal Light": Fumyō-kaku.

100 "Incomparable-Verse Valley": Zesshō-kei.

101 "Hall of the Guardian God": Reihi-byō.

102 "Hui-neng's Pond": Sōgen-chi.

103 "The Peak of the Held-Up Flower": Nenge-rei.

104 "The Bridge Where the Moon Crosses": Togetu-kyō.

105 "Three-Step Waterfall": Sankyū-gan.

106 "Cave of the Thousand Pines": Banshō-dō.

107 "Dragon-Gate House": Ryūmon-tei.

108 "Turtle Head Stūpa": Kichō-tō.

109 "Tiger Valley," *kokei* in Japanese: Kokei Reibun.

111 General Ashikaga Takauji's residence. The Three God Mountains: the three legendary mountains (P'eng-lai,

Fang-chang, and Ying-chou) of the ancient China where hermit gods live.

118 "Ox Turned Loose," *hōgo* in Japanese: Hōgo Kōrin.

119 "Clear Valley," *seikei* in Japanese: Seikei Tsūtetsu.

120 "Old Man at Leisure," *kansō* in Japanese: Kansō Shukan.

121 "Ancient Origin," *kogen* in Japanese: Kogen Shōgen.

122 "Old Man of Few Words," *mokuō* in Japanese: Mokuō Myōkai. Vimalakīrti, in the dialogue between Mañjushrī and himself concerning the dharma of nonduality, answers Mañjushrī with silence. In Zen this silence of his is compared to thunder.

123 "Jewel Cliff," *gyokugan* in Japanese: Ashikaga Motouji's dharma name.

124 "Joy Mountain," *zuizan* in Japanese: Ashikaga Yoshiakira's dharma name.

126 "Flat Mountain," *heizan* in Japanese: Heizan Zenkin.

127 "Beyond the World," *hōgai* in Japanese: Hōgai Kōon.

128 "Beyond Light," *zesshō* in Japanese: Zesshō Chikō.

129 "Hut in Harmony," *tekian* in Japanese: Tekian Hōjun.

130 The civil war (1336–1392) refers to the war between the two Ashikaga brothers, Takauji and Tadayoshi.

List of Names in Musō's Poems

After each name, occurrences in the text are noted by poem number. Traditionally, Musō Soseki has been called Musō Kokushi; "kokushi" is an honorific title, "Teacher of the Nation." "Oshō" and "Zenji" are also honorific titles to Zen masters, though priests are generally called "Oshō" today.

Ashikaga Motouji (1340–1367): one of Takauji's sons. (123)

Ashikaga Tadayoshi (1306–1352): Ashikaga Takauji's brother. (Intro, 73, 85)

Ashikaga Takauji (1305–1358): founder of the Muromachi Shogunate (1336–1573). (Intro, 75, 111)

Ashikaga Yoshiakira (1330–1367): one of Takauji's sons and the second general of the Muromachi Shogunate. (124)

Bukkō Zenji: Mugaku Sogen or Wu-hsueh Tsu-yuan (1226–1286): Chinese Zen master. Came to Japan and became the founder of Engaku-ji in Kamakura. Dharma grandfather. (90)

Chao-chou: Chao-chou Ts'ung-shen (778–897): Chinese Zen master. (6)

Daisen Oshō: Daisen Dōtsū (1265–1339): dharma friend. (8)

Dōgen: Eihei Dōgen (1201–1253): founder of the Japanese Sōtō Zen; famous for his *Shōbō Genzo* (*The Eye and Treasury of the True Law*). (Intro)

Dompō Shūō (D. 1401): disciple. (94)

Gassan Shūsū (1331–1399): disciple. (35)

Gen: Kosen Ingen (1295–1374): dharma friend. Studied in Yuan China. (42, 79)

Gen'nō Oshō: Gen'nō Hongen (1281–1332): dharma brother. (31)

Gidō Shūshin (1325–1388): major disciple. (63)

Go-Daigo (1288–1339): emperor. (Intro, 22)

Gyokuen (dates unknown): Hosokawa Yoriyuki's wife. (71)

Gyokugan: see Ashikaga Motouji. (123)

Heizan Zenkin (dates unknown): disciple. (126)

Hōgai Kōon (D. 1363): disciple. (127)

Hōgo Kōrin (D. 1373): dharma friend. Studied in Yuan China. (118)

Hosokawa Yoriyuki (1329–1392): warrior and feudal lord. (70)

Hsiang-yen: Hsiang-yen Chih-hsien (D. 898): Chinese Zen master. Attained satori at the sound of a stone hitting a bamboo stalk. (21)

Huang-lung: Huang-lung Hui-nang (1002–1069): Chinese Zen master. (51)

Hui-neng: Hui-neng Ta-chien (638–713): the Sixth Patriarch. Lived at Ts'ao Valley. Chinese. (Intro, 102)

Iku: Genshō Shūiku (1321–1386): disciple. Studied in Yuan China. (44)

Issan Kokushi: I-shan I-ning (1248–1317): Chinese Zen master. Visited Japan and lived at Kenchō-ji and Engaku-ji. (Intro)

Kan: Tsūsō Kōkan (dates unknown): disciple. (43)

Kansō Shukan (dates unknown): disciple. (120)

Keigan: see Hosokawa Yoriyuki. (70)

Kengai Oshō: Kengai Kōan (1252–1331): dharma friend. (34)

Kihō Shiyū (dates unknown): disciple. (27)

Ko: Reigaku Sōko (dates unknown): dharma friend. Studied in Yuan China. (98)

Kōan Fushō (dates unknown): disciple. (48)

Koboku Jōei (dates unknown): disciple. (25)

Kogen Shōgen (D. 1364): dharma friend. Studied in Yuan China. (121)

Kōgon (1313–1364): emperor. Became a Zen priest after retirement. (64)

Kōhō Ken'nichi: see Bukkō Zenji. (Intro)

Kokei Reibun (dates unknown): disciple. (109)

Kosan: see Ashikaga Tadayoshi. (73)

Kyūō Fukan (1321–1410): disciple. Studied in Yuan China. (26)

Lin Hsiang-ru (third century B.C.E.): famous statesman in the old China. (19)

Lin-chi: Lin-chi I-hsuan (D. 867): Chinese Zen master, founder of the Rinzai (Lin-chi) sect. (60)

Ma-tsu: Ma-tsu Tao-i (707–786): Chinese Zen master. (39)

Meghashri: fictitious character appearing in the Hua-yen (Kegon) sutra; one of the fifty-three saints and the first person visited by Sudhana. (20)

Mokuan Shūyu (1318–1373): disciple. (72)

Mokuō Myōkai (dates unknown): disciple. (122)

Mugoku Oshō: Mugoku Shigen (1282–1359): major disciple. (74, 113)

Muhan: see Kōgon. (64)

Myō: Mōzan Chimyō (1292–1366): dharma uncle. (80, 81)

Nang-yang: Nan-yang Hui-chung (D. 775): Chinese Zen master. (44)

Ninzan: see Ashikaga Takauji. (75)

Old Man Ho: see Chao-chou. (34, 69)

Reizan Oshō: Reizan Dōin or Ling-shan Tao-yin (1255–1325): Chinese Zen master and dharma friend. Came to Japan in 1320. (5, 6, 7)

Sagami Umenokami (dates unknown): minister of horses. (47)

Seikei Tsūtetsu (1300–1385): disciple. Studied in Yuan China. (119)

Seisetsu Shōchō: Ch'ing-cho Cheng-ch'eng (1274–1339): Chinese Zen master. Came to Japan in 1326. (40)

Shen-kuan: Hui-k'o (487–593): name of the Second Patriarch

in his younger days. Showed his earnest wish to become Bodhidharma's disciple by cutting off one of his arms. (68, 77)

Shō: Kasan Sōshō (dates unknown): possibly a disciple. (83)

Shōzan Shūnen (dates unknown): disciple. (39)

Shun'oku Myōha (1311–1388): major disciple. Edited the *West Mountain Evening Talk*. (95)

Sohō Pō (dates unknown): disciple. (46)

Subhūti (dates unknown): the one of Shākyamuni's Ten Disciples who best understood emptiness. (30, 70)

Sudhana: fictitious young boy in the Hua-yen sutra. Visits fifty-three saints seeking instruction and meets Meghashri first. (20, 99)

Sūzan Oshō: Sūzan Kochū (1276–1345): dharma friend. Studied in Yuan China. (76, 77, 114)

Taihei Oshō: Taihei Myōjun (1276–1327): dharma brother and one of Musō's best friends. (4, 11)

Tan-hsia: Tan-hsia T'ien-jan (739–824): Chinese Zen master. (15)

Tekian Hōjun (dates unknown): disciple. (129)

Tengan Oshō: Tengan Ekō (1273–1335): dharma brother. Studied in Yuan China. (49)

Tetsu: Daidō Myōtetsu (dates unknown): dharma brother. (82)

Unzan Chietsu (dates unknown): dharma friend. (41)

Vimalakīrti (dates unknown): lay Buddhist in the days of Shākyamuni. The protagonist of the Vimalakīrti sūtra. (122)

Zesshō Chikō (dates unknown): disciple. (128)

Zuizan: see Ashikaga Yoshiakira. (124)

About the Author

W.S. Merwin was born in New York City in 1927 and grew up in Union City, New Jersey and in Scranton, Pennsylvania. From 1949 to 1951 he worked as a tutor in France, Mallorca, and Portugal. He has since lived in many parts of the world, most recently on Maui in the Hawaiian Islands. His many books of poems, prose, and translations include *The Folding Cliffs: A Narrative* (Knopf, 1998), *Flower & Hand* (Copper Canyon Press, 1997), *The Second Four Books of Poems* (Copper Canyon Press, 1993), and *The Rain in the Trees* (Knopf, 1988). He has been the recipient of many awards and prizes, including the Fellowship of the Academy of American Poets (of which he is now a Chancellor), the Pulitzer Prize in Poetry, and the Bollingen Prize in Poetry; most recently he has received the Governor's Award for Literature of the state of Hawaii, the Tanning Prize for mastery in the art of poetry, a Lila-Wallace–Reader's Digest Writer's Award, and the Ruth Lilly Poetry Prize.

ABOUT ONE HUNDRED YEARS after Musō wrote his last poem, Nicolas Jenson was cutting type punches for the busy publishing trade in Venice. His letters retain the pen-drawn details of calligraphy. Specimens of Jenson's work have inspired many typeface designs, including the face used in this book, Adobe Jenson, created for digital composition by Robert Slimbach in 1995. Book design and composition by Valerie Brewster, Scribe Typography. Front cover design by John D. Berry.

✦ ✦ ✦

9 781556 590917